AGRARIAN SYSTEM OF KASHMIR
(1846 – 1889)

Agrarian System of Kashmir
(1846–1889)

R.L. Hangloo

COMMONWEALTH PUBLISHERS
NEW DELHI (INDIA)

FIRST EDITION, 1995

ISBN 81-7169-351-2

Published by: Ajay Verma for Commonwealth Publishers, 4378/4-B, Gali Murari Lal, Ansari Road, Darya Ganj, New Delhi-110 002 Ph.: 3272541

Typesetted by: S.P. PRINTECH, G-19, Vijay Chowk, Laxmi Nagar, Delhi-110 092, Ph.: 2214076

Printed by: Efficient Offset Printers, 215, Shahzada Bagh, Industrial Complex, Phase II, Delhi-110 035

Preface

In the recent past the economic history has attracted the attention of historians all over the world. In India too subjects like agrarian structure, peasant communities, rural societies, trade, industries and other aspects of Indian society and economy were chosen for study by various scholars. But in the field of such studies Kashmir remained by and large untouched.

It is background of this void that I chose to study agrarian system of Kashmir under Dogras from 1846 upto 1889. The problems were many and varied, for it was extremely difficult to measure any sort of economic change for this period and to understand its significance without the availability of regular contemporary records, like price index's, population figures, production figures, average size of holdings and productivity. It was, therefore, with considerable relief that manuscript sources like the 13 volume *(Akhbarat)* of Mirza Saif-ud-din, *Tarikh-i-Hassan* of Peer Hassan Shah and *Kaifiyat-i-Intizam-i-mulk-i-Kashmir of Ramju Dhar*, among others came to my rescue and yielded considerable and reliable information on some of these aspects. The study has generally been based on contemporary manuscripts, records, land *Pattas*, administrative reports, settlement reports, *Dasturl-amals* and contemporary official correspondence which is mostly available in the National Archives of India, the Jammu & Kashmir state Archives at Jammu and Srinagar, and the

Punjab state Archives, Patiala. Besides I have made use of some unpublished reports, travel accounts, and published works.

For preparation of this book I express deep debt of gratitude to my teacher Prof. Harbans Mukhia for his exacting academic standards, unfailing guidance and very keen interest in my academic efforts despite his many academic and scholastic engagements. I am also grateful to Prof. S. Battacharya, Prof. Dilbag Singh, Prof. M.I. Khan, Prof. O.N. Koul, Dr. G.L. Koul and late Prof. Z.L. Jalla for their valuable suggestions and encouragement.

In terms of information, discussion and suggestions this book owes much to late Mirza Mohammad Afzal Beg (Ex-Revenue Minister of Jammu and Kashmir. I also thank Shree Jagar Nath Raina, President Zamindar Association District Anantnag and Shree Shivji Bhat Agrarian Reforms Commissioner Jammu and Kashmir (Retd.), they will immediately recognise the echo of various discussions we have had.

Lastly, I thank my wife Sharika who endured without complaint the difficulties that are bound to arise at home while bringing up our two children, Ark Prateem and Ark Pravah, without my regular assistance.

RATTAN LAL HANGLOO

Dedicated
to
My Grand Parents
Late Shree Pandit Goverdan Hangloo and Kakni

Content

1
Introduction

A study of the Agrarian System of Kashmir during the second half of the nineteenth century hardly needs any explicit justification in view of the predominantly rural character of the region.

Though the agrarian history of ancient and medieval India in general and of some regions in particular has been examined for a quite long time, little attention has been paid to the study of this problem in Kashmir's history. It is only a detailed study of various historical problems at regional level from epoch to epoch that can enable the scholars to make any wide level generalization about the character of Indian economy and society as a whole.[1]

Unfortunately most of the works dealing with the history of Kashmir for the above mentioned period appear

1. The character of the ancient and the medieval economy of India has been the subject of intense controversy amongst historians. Thus while D.D. Kosambi and R.S. Sharma have argued for the characterization of a long period of Indian history as feudal, Irfan Habib has questioned the utility of this notion for Indian history. More recently Harbans Mukhia has made a detailed critique of the concept of Indian feudalism and has suggested the notion of a free peasant economy in medieval India, a notion defined very differently from the one already in circulation. See D.D. Kosambi, *Introduction to the Study of Indian History*, Bombay 1956, pp. 296-405. R.S. Sharma *Indian Feudalism*, Calcutta 1965, Irfan Habib, "The social distribution of landed property in pre-British India" *Indian Society, Historical Probings*, edited by R.S. Sharma, Delhi 1974, pp. 264-316. Harbans

(Contd. to next page)

to be somewhat unsatisfactory from the point of view of our problem. The first among such works was *Gulabnama* written in 1865 by Dewan Kripa Ram, the then Prime Minister of Kashmir.[2] It was written under the supervision of Maharaja Ranbir Singh, the son and successor of Maharaja Gulab Singh. It has been written in the typically ornate Persian style of the 19th century. The author mainly extolled the virtues of Gulab Singh.

Like wise the other works written on Maharaja Gulab Singh and Maharaja Ranbir Singh's period (1846-1885 A.D.) are either biographical or by and large political in nature. Seldom if ever is there a reference to any social and economic problems of the time in them.[3]

(Contd. from previous page)

Mukhia, "Was there Feudalism in Indian History", *'Journal of Peasant Studies*, Vol. VIII, No. 3, April 1981, pp. 273-310.
However, it is evident that there would be considerable regional variations in the pattern of development and that a careful analysis of the economy of each region is necessary for an evaluation of agrarian economy of the country as a whole for any period.

2. Dewan Kripa Ram hailed from the eminent Dewan family of Eminabad. They had, from the commencement of Maharaja Gulab Singh's reign, practically monopolised the office of the Dewan. He became the Dewan of Maharaja Ranbir Singh at the age of 24 in 1857 and he held the office of Dewan till his death in 1876. L.H. Griffin, *The Punjab Chiefs*, Lahore, 1805, pp. 131-32.
3. The other works include *Biography of Maharaja Gulab Singh* by Pandit Salig Ram Koul, Srinagar, 1923: *Gulab Singh, the founder of Jammu and Kashmir State* by Sardar K.M. Panikar, London, 1930; *The building of Jammu and Kashmir State being an achievement of Maharaja Gulab Singh*, by A.N. Sapru, Lahore 1931; *The Jammu fox, a Biography of Maharaja Gulab Singh*, by S.S. Bawa, London, 1974; *Maharaja Ranbir Singh* (a vernacular biography) by N.D. Nargis, Jammu, 1921. *Tarikh-i- Dogradesh* (Urdu) by N.D. Nargis, Jammu, 1965. *Kashmir-aur-Dogra Raj*, (Urdu) by Fazl Hussain. Srinagar 1979. A recent work is *Maharaja Gulab Singh* (unpublished Ph. D. thesis submitted in 1977 to Kashmir University by Phool Pyari Mam. But she has also failed to examine some of the important aspects of economic development like agriculture, trade and industry during Maharaja Gulab Singh's period.

During Maharaja Pratap Singh's reign W.R. Lawrence produced a detailed work on the socio-economic and political aspects of Kashmirs history form the earlist times to his day, but in his work the exposition of basic concepts is not sufficiently clear and accurate, to enable us to use them in considering the agrarian and the rural problem.[4]

Another recent work is that of Dr. M.L. Kapoor, which is "a study in socio-economic life of people during Maharaja Pratap Singh's period (1885-1925 A.D.)" but the agrarian system of the State of even Kashmir finds no place in it. In the treatment of socio-economic history, the author has not gone beyond the traditional method of giving a general description of the masses. In dealing with society he has confined himself to a description of the dress, food and pastimes. The social stratification has been discussed in terms of differences in peoples dress and food habits. The author has not made use of the Persian sources of the time which perhaps explains the reason for the limited scope of this work.[5]

---

4. W.R. Lawrence, *Valley of Kashmir*, London, 1895. Mr. Lawrence took over as the land-settlement Commissioner of Kashmir from the year 1889. He undertook the land reforms at the time when the Indians in all provinces were demanding radical agrarian reforms and modernization of agriculture. But the utmost honesty that was required to make the settlement a success did not exist. Being an agent of colonial regime he than relieved the peasantry of Kashmir of the problems of poverty and settlement of their holdings. Besides his sudden departure from Kashmir in 1895 also left the settlement of holdings incomplete.
5. M.L. Kapoor, *Social and Economic History of Jammu and Kashmir from 1885-1925 A.D.*, an unpublished Ph. D. thesis approved by Jammu University in 1974. Recently M.I. Khan has published a valuable work on the history of Srinagar. Though the author does not offer the reader an analysis of the socio-economic problems of Kashmir as a whole, he has made penetrating analysis of such problems of the city of Srinagar. The varied problems studied therein appear to have determined the direction of the evolution of the social and economic structure of the city as also the formation of various economic units and their relation with the various classes of society from time to time.

In order to understand the process of evolution of society, one must examine this process at its lowest end. One must, in other words, carefully examine what changes, if any, were occuring in the manner in which the peasant cultivated his field and the manner in which produce was distributed among various sections of society. It is this aspect which the recent historical research has thrown up as the most important and I have taken it up in context of Kashmir's history.

The people inhabiting the territory of Kashmir have played an important role in history from earliest times and survived the conditions—the isolation from the countries of both east and west caused by its strategic and geographical location as well as the nature of political intervention by the regions ruling class which had made her development extremely slow till the end of the 19th century.

As early as 1586 Kashmir was linked to the Mughal Empire. The establishment of Mughal rule in the conquered province of Kashmir was an event of great significance, since it brought certain basic changes in economic relations amongst the various classes of the agricultural community.[6] Emperor Akbar effected the new rules and regulations with

---

6. In ancient and early medieval period the situation in Kashmir was particularly bad. The people had suffered under the Hindu and muslim rulers when large number of them had been annihilated. There was no regular system of a assessment and collection. The usual political feuds among nobles exposed the valley to the menacing neighbours like Turks and Mughals. This led to more and more economic decline of the valley, political fragmentation of the nobility and ultimately in 1586 the valley fell in the hands of Mughal rulers, *Baharistan-i-Shahi,* (Anonymous) Persian Manuscript Srinagar Research Department library folios 182b and 183 b. (Henceforth ff. for folios) Suka and Prajayabhata, *Rajvalipatika* Sanskrit Ms. English tr. by J.C. Dutt.' under the title *Kings of Kashmira* (3 Vols.), Calcutta 1935, Vol. III, p. 407.

regard to land revenue system of Kashmir.[7] But before his successors could achieve the economic and political objects of their rule, symptoms of decay began to manifest at the centre and ultimately the valley was taken over by the Afghan rulers in 1753.[8]

The chief concern of the Afghan rulers too remained the grasping and realisation by quick and oppressive methods of as much of the agricultural produce as possible. Neither new regulations were introduced nor the old ones were kept intact. There followed a complete breach of laws and violation of the scheduled revenue rates in Kashmir. In course of time the gradual disintegration of central administration took place and the provincial governors appointed by the Afghans became more or less independent.[9] Taking advantage of the weakness at the centre various intermediaries also engaged in a scramble for obtaining territorial possession and control over their respective areas.[10] The already discontended massess were ready to welcome any political shift that could replace the Afghan rule (1753-1819 A.D.). A group of nobility headed by Beer Bal Dhar broke away from the Afghans and settled the matters with the Sikh rulers in Punjab in the second decade of 19th century.[11]

It was, therefore, in 1819 that the doubly oppressed subjects of the territory of Kashmir passed into the hands of Ranjit Singh. There was a change in the administrative

---

7. Abul Fazl, *Ain-i-Akbari*, persian 3 Vols. Vol. II, English tr. by colonel H.S. Jarret, 3rd ed. 1978, p. 366. See Vol. I, p. 347.
8. Ramjudhar, *Kaifiat-i-Intizam-i-mulk-i-Kashmir*, unpublished (Persian Ms.) Research Department Library, Srinagar, ff. 3-4.
9. *Ibid*. See also, Lawrence, *Valley of Kashmir*, Srinagar, 1895, p. 196. R K. Parmu, *A History of Muslim Rule in Kashmir* (1320-1819), Delhi, 1969, pp. 352-353.
10. Ramjudhar, *op.cit.*, f. 4.
11. Parmu, *op.cit.*, pp. 385-387.

structure of Kashmir which also led to a change in the land-based relations between various classes of society.[12]

However, these changes did not affect the methods of cultivation nor did they lead to an economic renaissance, though they did change the condition of the peasantry for worse. By and large the Mughal system was followed. The Sikh administrative system did not prove worthy of its expectations. The administration at the hands of Sikh governors became quite lax.

Like their Afghan predecessors they did not miss any opportunity of misappropriating revenue.[13] Many additional *abwabs* and cesses were allowed to be imposed besides the usual revenue.[14] The intermediaries considered themselves free to impose any cesses or *abwabs* on the peasants without the concurrence of the State.[15] Large portions of peasants income was taken away in rents, high interest charges and taxes. Unfair terms of price exchange also left the peasants with such little subsistence that it was neither possible for them to improve their farms nor to raise their living standards.[16]

In the first half of the 19th century the British colonial masters became more conscious of the mounting danger of Russia from north western side to their Indian colony. As a result they began to think in terms of liquidation of the Sikh

---

12. Dewan Krishen Lal's *Account of Kashmir,* Foreign secret consultation, 31 March, 1848, file no. 68. National Archives of India (Henceforth N.A.I).
13. H. M. Lawrence, *Transfer of Government to Maharaja Gulab Singh,* Section C, 28 January 1848, file no's 33-34, Jammu Archives.
14. *Ibid.*
15. *Ibid.*
16. Whether the increase in various taxes meant a real rise in tax burden on the peasantry, is no doubt a difficult question to answer because the sources do not provide us with income data. However, attempt has been made to measure the incidence of the taxes levied.

empire which could not only transfer to them the economic resources of Sikh empire but also provide them with some of the important borders which were indispensable for safeguarding their Indian colony.[17] In course of time the Sikh principalities between the rivers Sutlej and Jamuna passed under the protection and care of the British. The Anglo-Sikh wars followed in 1845-46 in which the British came out victorious and in the process of setting the political future of occupied territories and their autonomous vassals and chiefs, they handed over Jammu and Kashmir to Maharaja Gulab Singh as their vassal in 1846.[18]

---

17. Charles Hardinge, *Viscount Hardinge*, Oxford, 1900, p. 133. *See also letters from Sir Hentry Hardinge to Queen Victoria*, 18th of Feb. 1846. Foreign and Pol. Deptt. file no. 66 N.A.I. F. Young husband, *Kashmir* Edinburgh, 1909, pp. 168-172. This attitude of British was expressed by M.B. Bayley to Hob House in this letter dated January 1841 "Even if the holding of a force in Afghanistan should be necessary for their maintenance we should find in the resources of Punjab, resources necessary for their maintenance, we should reinforce them without any difficulty and with Kashmere on our flank. The whole line of Indus in our possession, we might defy all attacks whether from European or Asiatic enemies". S.S. Bawa, *The Jammu Fox*, London, 1974, p. 88. In course of time the Sikh principalities between river Sutlej and Jammu passed under the protection and care of British. The Anglo Sikh wars followed in 1845-46 in which British came out victorious and in the process of settling the political future of the occupied territories and their autonomous vassals they handed over the Jammu and Kashmir to Gulab Singh in 1846. H.M. Lawrence, *Transfer of Government to Maharaja Gulab Singh*, Section C, 28 January 1848. File nos. 33-44. Jammu Archives. Karl Marx also mentions that when British army entered Lahore in triumph on February 20, 1846 it appears that there was no money in the treasury for the payment of $ 150,000 to Sikh soldiers. Hardinge declared the annexation of Kashmir to company but when Gulab Singh offered to pay the money, Kashmir was made over to him. This was how Hardinge paid the war expenses to troops of Khalsa army. Karl Marx *Notes on Indian History*, Moscow, 1988 (reprint), p. 142.
18. H.M. Lawrence, *op.cit.*, Section C 28 January 1848, File Nos. 33-44, Jammu Archives.

Although the year 1846 also brought a change in the administration as a result of the establishment of Jammu and Kashmir state under Maharaja Gulab Singh yet the condition of Kashmir continued to be as it had been under the Sikhs.[19] Though during this period the frequent land settlements were carried out in other parts of the country and it was understood that the settlement would lead to more rapid accumulation of capital in agriculture and its consequent improvement but Kashmir was still passing through a traditional economic order because of its geographical isolation from the rest of India.

There was an increasing neglect of the rural economic infrastructure, the transport, irrigation and flood control systems through corrupt and inept bureaucratic management. All these developments interacted to produce rather alarming consequences for the agrarian economy. The distribution of land had become more and more unequal, pressure on peasants to migrate became more intense, and the landless peasants became an almost inexhaustible source of manpower for the landlords and the State officials for carrying out *Begar* (corvee).[20]

Thus the agrarian structure of the period under review was a matter of comprehensive interest affecting all sections of society. There were conflicting interests of *jagirdars, pattadars, chakdars* and other segments of peasantry who made up all social classes in a variety of ways.

No pure and simple landlord class existed and *chakdars* were numerous. Although high officials and the Maharaja agreed that the greatest rewards in society must go to agriculturalist, but they concerned themselves more with the raising of taxes. The Maharajas all in their turn appear

---

19. F. Younghusband, *op.cit.*, pp. 175-179.
20. Mirza Saif-ud-Din, *Akhbarat*, 13 Vols. (Persian Ms.) Research Department Library, Srinagar, Kashmir, Vol. I, f. 74.

to have been too preoccupied with the western penetration to introduce any thing new and settled in the field of agriculture.[21]

Consequently few in the class of peasants could escape the distress and depression from the country side in the form of mounting indebtedness, forced labour, and the rising number of landless peasants and workers.

Hence the study of agrarian structure of Kashmir involves a number of aspects. These include:

(*i*) The impact of the ecology on the agrarian economy of Kashmir.

(*ii*) The extent of cultivation and the changes, if any, in the cropping pattern.

(*iii*) The agricultural production for use and for sale.

(*iv*) The nature of agricultural technology.

(*v*) The nature and extent of revenue assignments, grants and the position of assignees and grantees in rural society.

(*vi*) The nature of revenue administration, its organisation and functioning.

(*vii*) The magnitude of the land revenue demand and its impact on the condition of peasantry.

(*viii*) Other subsidiary occupations of peasantry which supplemented their income.[22]

All these aspects are closely related and require a detailed study. However, after an examination of the sources it has not been possible at present to answer all

---

21. A.P. Nicholson, *Scrapes of paper, India's broken treaties, her princes and her problem*, London 1930, pp. 88-90.
22. The study of the above mentioned aspects is confined to the agrarian system of Kashmir valley only and not the State of Jammu and Kashmir as a whole. The State of Jammu and Kashmir consists of three regions, Jammu, Kashmir and Ladakh which have little in common more than a mere political destiny.

these questions satisfactorily. The paucity of statistical data, with regard to population, production and holdings involved a great deal of difficulty in making out some generalisations which could prove fruitful.

The burden of the present study is to identify purely in a descriptive manner, the agricultural production of Kashmir, the nature of cropping pattern and the technology used, the methods of assessment and collection, the magnitude of land revenue demand, the revenue machinery its nature and functioning.

Besides attention has also been focussed on the land revenue assignees and land grantees. The condition of the peasantry and the pattern of trade has also been looked into.

Like all descriptive works, this book also suffers from inevitable shortcomings. Because it is only a step towards a fuller understanding of the agrarian economy of Kashmir in all its comprehensiveness. In fact I had intended to do much further research on this subject before publishing it but the crisis which overtook Kashmir made that impossible. The study must therefore stand as it is, with only minimal changes, in the hope that inspite of its imperfections it will be of use to future scholars, and stimulate them to carry on where I left off.

2
Agricultural Production

The territories of Jammu and Kashmir State which are almost entirely mountainous, occupy a unique position in the topography of the Indian sub-continent. They vary in height from hillocks on the Punjab border to the great Himalayan and Kara-Koram ranges. Among these mountains the vale of Kashmir is a level plain.[1]

Though owing to this mountainous character of the valley of Kashmir the area of land under cultivation has

---

1. Mountains of Kashmir constitute a very prominent feature of Kashmir's geography. They together constitute the sources of water. These mountains lend a peculiar scenic beauty to Kashmir. But whereas they ensure the defence of Kashmir they also have been the cause of its isolation from the rest of the world. M.A. Stein, *Ancient Geography of Kashmir,* Calcutta, 1899, pp. 24-27. C.E. Bates, *Gazetteer of Kashmir and adjacent Districts of Kashtwar, Badrawah, Jammu and Noshera, Punch and the Valley of Kishen Ganga,* Calcutta, 1873, pp. 1-3. F. Drew, *Jammu and Kashmir Territories,* London, 1875, pp. 9-13. Peer Hassan Shah, *Tarikh-i-Hasan* (Persian), Vol. I., Srinagar, 1885, pp. 3-7. A.N. Raina, *Geography of Jammu and Kashmir State,* Delhi 1971, pp. 1-24.

been very small, the character of economy throughout the period of our study has remained agrarian.[2]

(*a*) Crop Pattern

The peculiar physical character and the climate has from times past, been a serious handicap to intensive farming and diversification of crops in the valley. The land remained under snow for four to five months a year when no cultivation was possible at all. As a result rice was the main *Kharif* crop but after its harvest late in September and October there was very little time left to sow another crop.[3] Of all the *Rabi* crops only such crops were sown, after the *Kharif* season, whose germination took place before the snow fall and the plants started growing, after the snow had melted, in the month of March and April. The *Rabi* crops which took four to five months to mature—in other parts of the country took five to six months in the valley of Kashmir.[4] Since *Kharif* was harvested by September/ October *i.e.* on the eve of snowfall, and since there was little time to prepare the soil for the next crops, *Rabi* seeds were

---

2. The sources are silent about the details of the total cultivable area and the area under cultivation during the period under study. Dewan Krishen Lal observes that the total area of land in Kashmir was 750,000 acres out of which 200,000 acres were under water. 150,000 acres under forest and hills, 50,000 acres under the roads and 350,000 acres was cultivable. See *Foreign Deptt. Sec. 31st March 1848*, file nos. 60-77, National Archives of India (NAI).
3. From March to September ploughing, transplantation, weeding and harvesting took place and it was during this period that peasants were often taken away from their lands for *Begar* (forced labour) and lands were not tilled properly. See Mirza Saif-ud-Din, *Akhbarat* (Persian Ms.) (1846-57 A.D.), Vol. IV, ff. 61,78,84, Research Department Library, Srinagar, Kashmir. See also Charles Girdlestone, *Memorandom on Kashmir*, Calcutta, 1973, p. 35.
4. Lawrence, *Valley*, pp. 325-330; *Imperial Gazetteer of India*, Vol. XV (From Karachi to Kotayam), Oxford, 1908, pp. 115-117.

sown only in such fields as had not been cultivated during the *Kharif* season.[5] And since *Rabi* crops took longer to mature in Kashmir, they left no time for the *Kharif*. In effect therefore Kashmir's peasants had to subsist on a one-crop economy, either *Rabi* or *Kharif*.

The important *Kharif* and *Rabi* crops are given in the following table.[6]

KHARIF CROPS	*RABI CROPS*
Rice	Wheat
Maize	Barley
Cotton	Tibet Barley
Saffron	Opium, poppy
Tobacco	Rape
Millet	Flax
Amranthus	Beans (Viciafaba)
Buckwheat	
Pulses	
Sesame	

In spite of the obvious advantages of the system of crop rotation, the farmers generally preferred the cultivation of rice when adequate irrigation facilities were available. They allowed land to remain lea in times of deficiency of irrigation and knew that their labour would not be repaid if they sowed other crops.[7] Furthermore, the small quantities

---

5. F. Drew, *The Northern Barrier of India*, London, 1877, pp. 172-173. See Lawrence, *Valley*, pp. 325-330.
   Lawerence, *Valley*, pp. 325-330. See *A Note on Jammu* and Kashmir (Published by Jammu and Kashmir State), Jammu, 1928, pp. 27-29.
6. Lawrence, *Valley*, pp. 325-330.
7. F. Younghusband, *Kashmir* Edinburgh, 1909, p.78.
   W.R. Lawrence, *Assessment Report of Uri-Tehsil*, Jammu, 1898, p. 4.
   The other crops included cotton, mash, barley and maize. W.R. Lawrence, *Assessment Report of Baramulla Tehsil*, Jammu, 1905, p. 9.

of commercial crops grown in the state afforded little scope for agrobased industries.

The Kashmiri peasant believed that the note of Cuckoo heralded the time of snowing. For rice, peasants practised two systems of cultivation. Under the first rice was grown broadcast; under the second rice was first sown in a nursery and then transplanted.[8] The broadcast system involved much labour because it needs more ploughings than nursery system and was fairly unproductive. In comparison the nursery system was in greater vogue.[9] The broadcast rice had to be sown earlier and required more watering, more weeding and intensive labour.[10] Regular weeding was carried out in case of rice cultivation, maize and cotton crops.[11] Both men and women did transplantation but the ploughing operations, broadcast sowing, reaping and weeding operations were carried out by men alone.[12] In rice

8. Report of British Empire Exhibition, Jammu and Kashmir, London, 1924, pp. 20-23.
9. *Tarikh-i-Kalan* (Persian Ms.) (Anonymous) M/1004 Punjab Archives Patiala, f. 201 See W.W.H. Greatheds Impressions about Kashmir as contained in an extract from a letter dated October 26, 1871 from Naitintal as cited in Charles Girdleston, *Memorandom on Kashmir*, Appendix D.
10. The chief problem in weeding arose from the automatic germination of seeds left behind from the previous harvest. The difficulty was overcome by alternately growing rice of green and other coloured straws. So that any left out rice plant could be easily detected and pulled out. Lawrence, *Valley*, pp. 325-327. *A note on Jammu and Kashmir*, p. 28.
11. G.T. Vigne, *Travels in Kashmir, Ladakh, Iskardu countries adjoining the mountain course of Indus and Himalayan, North of Punjab*, Vol. I, London, 1842, p. 310. See E.F. Neve, *Beyond the Pirpanjal*, London, 1915, pp. 59-60. Hargopal Koul Khasta, *Guldasta-i-Kashmir* (Urdu), Lahore, 1883, p. 79.
12. This fact is borne out by a drawing of the mid 19th century Kashmir; see illustration No.1 following p. 16. The drawing is in India Office Library, London. My Supervisor, Professor Harbans Mukhia of

(Contd. to next page)

cultivation weeding was done with hands and feet. There were no special implements.[13] In case of maize it was done with hands and hoe.[14] In case of weeding the peasant was very alert and kept strict watch over certain insects which caused havoc to the young plants of rice.[15]

Agriculture in Kashmir depended much on the timely arrival of monsoon and due to the uncertainty of weather there was a considerable seasonal variation in production levels.[16] However, in the scheme of agriculture food crops occupied the most significant place.

Moreover, cultivation was not possible for the greater part of the year due to the given climate which rendered double cropping more difficult. In order to evaluate the significance of agriculture in the economy of Kashmir we discuss below some of the most important crops then cultivated.

(Contd. from previous page)

Jawaharlal Nehru University, New Delhi, has been kind enough to provide me this and some other illustrations for my use from his collection of the photographs of the drawings. Though the *British Empire Exhibition* states that the transplantation was carried out by women alone and the men used to distribute seedlings but the illustration from the aforesaid drawing exhibits both men and women transplanting seedlings. See illustration No. 1. p. 16.

13. See also illustration No. 1. During the weeding operations the peasants suffered from Eruption (Khaz) caused by the continual immerson of the parts of their body in water. Their ankles and wrists were affected but hands and feet escaped relatively undamaged owing to the protection provided by mud. The peasants used to apply the *Kelmtil*, oil which was extracted from pine and mixed with ghee, to the affected parts of the body. C.E. Bates, *Gazetteer*, pp. 14-18.
14. Dewan Kripa Ram, *Gulzar-i-Kashmir* (Persian) Lahore, 1870, p. 486. The original manuscript is available in National Archives, New Delhi. Lawrence, *Valley*, pp. 325-327.
15. See, *A Note on Jammu and Kashmir*, p. 28.
16. W.R. Lawrence, *Imperial Gazetteer of India Provincial Series Jammu and Kashmir*, Calcutta, 1909, p. 20.
    Guyhunter, *Modernizing Peasant Societies*, London, 1968, p. 87.
    F. Drew, *Northern Barrier of India*, pp. 170-173.

Illustration I

Rice

Being the staple food of the inhabitants, it was the principal crop cultivated in Kashmir. It accounted for three fourths of the cultivable area during the Sikh period.[17] According to Dewan Krishen Lal the total cultivable area in 1848 A.D. was 350,000 acres.[18] However, rice cultivation was confined to the flat portion of the Valley with alluvial soil, where water could reach with ease and in plenty. It required warm moist climate which was characteristic of this portion.[19] The quantity of seed sown per acre was twenty to twentyfour seers and the out turn varied from five to thirty *Kharwars*.[20] In hilly areas where rice was grown the out turn was of a lower order and the rice was also of inferior quality. In Kashmir ninety four varieties of rice were grown.[21] Among

---

17. G.T. Vigne, *Travels*, Vol. I., p. 309. There was no systematic method of measuring land with some instrument. In Kashmir land was measured according to the quantity of seed sown, per acre the extent of ground which required one *Kharwar* of seed. As a unit of land one *Kharwar* of land was equal to thirty two *kanals* or four acres. Mir Ahmed, *Dastural Amal-i-Kashmir*, (Persian Ms.) M 829 Punjab State Archives Patiala, f. 133b. Mirza Saif-ud-Din, *Akhbarat*, Vol. I., f. 7. See *Diary of R.G. Taylor Punjab Government Records* (1847-49), Vol. VI, Lahore 1911-1915, p.31. Dewan Kripa Ram, *Gulzar-i-Kashmir*, pp. 256-57.
18. Dewan Krishen Lal (*Account of Kashmir*), Foreign Deptt. Secret correspondence, March 31, 1848, File No. 66-77, N.A. I.
19. W.R. Lawrence, *Imperial Gazetteer*, pp. 49-50. A.N. Raina, *Geography of Jammu and Kashmir State*, pp. 100-101. See *Techno-Economic Survey of Jammu and Kashmir State*, NCAER, Delhi 1969, pp. 17-18.
20. Lawrence, *Valley*, p. 159.

    Gazetteer of Kashmir and Ladakh compiled under the direction of Quarter master general in India, the Intelligence Branch, Calcutta 1890, p. 59. The *Seer* and *Kharwar* were standard measures of weight then in vogue. The *seer* was of 21 *Chhataks* and *Kharwar* of sixteen *traks*; one *trak* was equal to five *seers*. Mir Ahmed, *op.cit.*, f. 133 b., Mirza, *op.cit.*, Vol. I., f. 7. Dewan Kripa Ram, *op.cit.*, pp. 256-57. See table on p. 28 which illustrates the input and out turn of various crops.

all these varieties *Kunjidanyi, Basmat* and *chogul* were considered the best. *Chogul* was grown in *pargana* Pakh.[22] Almost all lands under rice cultivation produced only one crop in the year and remained lea during winter when no cultivation was possible.[23]

Maize

In order of priority maize came next to rice. On the slopes, the uplands and all those areas in mountains where some amount of cultivation was possible, maize and pulses were grown. Generally the reclaimed swamps and peaty soils were suited to its cultivation. Besides the shepherds, cowherds and *Gujjars*, it was consumed by large sections of population in regions where little paddy was grown[24]. It needed, no regular irrigation; timely rains could help

---

21. Some of them are as follows *Larbyol, Mushkabudji, Lolianzun, Reban, Yimbirzal, Pothibrar, Sukhdas, Basmat, Shalkav, Braz, Zag-Danyi, Rani, Kunji-Dalni, Gurukoen, Chogul, Mokhtahal, Lachahal, Shahguzu Guru tanzi, Lal Krahna, Kenu Puthau, Nur, Karhana Shesher, Suirmal, Chata braz, Kamad, Tachitachee Mukhtabraz, Dudhakrid, Neka beyol, Barenbezol, Nihali, Bud Braz, Malwar, Chatazaz, Gurah, Ghunder, Chata newar, Kawhamah, Maitarahel, Babeer Mohiwan, Kawa Krihna, Keoziv, Moglubeyol, Chandahal, Sukal, Mohiaznun, Munkahashahd, Shalanzun, Oozulkrid, Baidanzun, Karalanzun, Bathal, Nekanzun Lenahzag, Nekahzag, Kranahzag, Basmat, Zazid Zekahtatar,* and *Talaibyol.* Kripa Ram, *Gulzar-i-Kashmir*, p. 278. Charles Girdlestone, *Memorandum on Kashmir*, Appendix C. See *Gazetteer of Kashmir and Ladakh*, p. 57.
22. Hargopal Koul Khasta, *Guldasta-i-Kashmir* (Urdu) Lahore 1883, pp. 20-22. *Gazetteer of Kashmir and Ladakh*, p. 57. Peer Hassan Shah also says about *Chogul*.

    "چُغل...که بربخ آنها بالنهایت ملایم وشیرین می شد"-

    "Chogul—among these is extremely soft and sweet." See Hasan, *Tarikh-i-Hasan*, Vol, I, p. 185.
23. F. Drew, *Northern Barrier of India*, pp. 170-173.
24. Lawrence, *Valley*, pp. 336-337. Lawrence, *Gazetteer*, pp. 49-50. A.N. Raina, *op.cit.*, p. 103.

TABLE 1

The following table shows a list of some crops of Kashmir with the amount of seed per acre, and the out turn per acre in the favourable years

Name of the crops in Kashmiri	*Name of the crops in Urdu*	*Seeds sown per acre*	*Maximum Produce*	
			Per Kharwar= 4 acres	*Per Acre*
Ushka	Jaw	Local Weight Seers 24	Kharwar 16	Kharwar 4
Kanak	Gehun	27	8	2
Tilgogal	Loriya	6	16	4
Masur	Masoor	12	6	$1\frac{1}{2}$
Kapas	Kapas	36	6	$1\frac{1}{2}$
Mung	Mung	12	10	$2\frac{1}{2}$
Mah	Mash	12	10	$2\frac{1}{2}$
Rajahmah	Lobia	12	10	$2\frac{1}{2}$
Dhan	Shali	22–24	10-60mds.	15
Makai	Makki	18	24	6
Tromba	Daraw	24	24	6
Ganhar	Swal	6	49	10

Sources : *Gazetteer of Kashmir and Ladakh*, Calcutta 1890. C.E. Bates, *A Gazetteer of Kashmir and adjoining districts of Kishtwar, Badarwah, Jammu Naoshera, Punch and the Valley of Kishen Ganga, Calcutta 1873.*
W.R. Lawrence, *Valley of Kashmir*, London 1895 and see also *Imperial Gazetteer of India, Provincial Series Jammu and Kashmir*, Calcutta, 1909.

produce bumper crops of maize. In the complete absence of rains crops would wither away. Soil and climate did not present much difficulty in its cultivation. The average production of maize per *Kharwar* of land was twenty four *Kharwars*.[25]

25. *Gazetteer of Kashmir and Ladakh*, pp. 61-62. Hassan,*op.cit*, Vol. I., p. 185.

Wheat

Topographically, Kashmir did not and still does not belong to the wheat growing regions of the sub-continent.[26] Nonetheless it did grow considerable amount of wheat next in importance only to maize. Certain specific areas were reserved for wheat cultivation. Its cultivation in Kashmir was mostly confined to Dachanpara and Khourpara *Parganas*.[27] It required a climate which is neither too warm nor too cold. Moreover, it does not need any atmospheric pressure or great deal of water for its cultivation. One *Kharwar* of land could produce eight *Kharwars* of wheat.[28]

Barley

It was grown throughout the valley on *barani* lands which were dependent on rain for moisture. The average production per *Kharwar* of land was sixteen *Kharwars*.[29] Another variety known as Tibetan barley was also cultivated in most hilly tracts of Kashmir. But it was cut before ripening and was used as fodder for cattle.[30]

Buck Wheat (Tromba)

It was grown in hilly tracts and depended very little on irrigation. It was of two varieties one called sweet *Tromba* and another white or Pinkish in colour.[31] The latter was often grown as a substitute for rice, in areas where water was scarce. It was mostly consumed in the form of porridge

---

26. R.L. Singh, *India, A Regional Geography*, Varanasi, 1971, pp. 347-361. A.N. Raina, *op.cit.*, p. 102.
27. *Tarikh-i-kalan* (Anonymous) f. 204.
28. *Gazetteer of Kashmir and Ladakh*, p. 61.
29. *Ibid*. See Lawrence, *Valley*, p. 338.
30. Hassan, *op.cit.*, Vol. I., p. 185. A.N. Raina, *op.cit.*, p. 102.
31. Lawrence, *Valley*, p. 338.

by the people inhabiting *kandi illagas i.e.*, hilly areas.[32]

Amranthus (Ganhar)

It was grown in cotton fields and also in the maize growing plots. It needed no irrigation or manure, with timely rains large our-turn was harvested. It was generally consumed by the Hindu population on the days of fast and on festive occasions.[33]

Kangni (Stariaitalica)

Kangni was a useful grain and was husked like rice but the people of Kashmir did not make much use of it because of its heating properties.[34] During the years when, adequate amount of water was not available most of lands were sown with *kangni*. A good harvest of *Kangni* needed two to four ploughings and careful weeding.[35] It was of two varieties one small and the other big. The former was generally consumed by the peasants and the latter was used for feeding cattle. Nothing at present is known about the seed sown per acre but the out turn was three maunds.[36]

Pulses

In some parts of Kashmir the cultivation of pulses co-existed with other crops including paddy and maize. The most popular pulses cultivated were *Mong, Moth, Mash* and *Rajmash*.[37] *Mong* was a *Kharif* crop and was entirely dependent on rain. The *banjar* lands could produce large quantities of this crop.[38]

---

32. *Ibid.* See also Lawrence, *Gazetteer*, p. 52. *Gazetteer of Kashmir and Ladakh*, p. 61.
33. Lawrence, *Valley*, p. 338.
34. *Ibid.*, p. 337.
35. *Ibid.*
36. *Ibid.*, pp. 337-338.
37. *Ibid.*, p. 337.
38. *Gazetteer of Kashmir and Ladakh*, pp. 60-64.

Moth (Phaselusa Conitifolous)

Among the pulses it was considered an inferior one and was generally used as fodder for cattle during winter.[39]

Mash (Phaseolus Rovburghu)

Its cultivation was extensively carried out in hilly areas. It was of two varieties, black and green. Both were consumed by the people. The last mentioned of the pulses, *Rajmash*, was of different varieties and was cultivated almost in every *pargana*. However, the consumption of pulses within the valley was not of the same order as in other parts of India.[40]

Besides the above mentioned crops Kashmir also produced a large quantity of waternuts and cash crops like cotton, tobacco, hopes, oilseeds and saffron.

Water nuts (Singharas)

Moorcraft who visited Kashmir in the early period of Sikh rule says that the average production of waternuts was about nine million six hundred and twenty thousand an loads and the total sale of *Singharas* was worth about Rs. 300,000 a year.[41] Ganeshi Lal who visited Kashmir during the initial period of Dogra rule observes that Rs. 25,000 are annually contributed to the Government revenue as the cess on *Singharas*.[42] Thus it is clear that *Singharas* were an important horticultural product of Kashmir.

---

39. Dewan Krishen Lal, *Account of Kashmir, Foreign Deptt.* See March 31, 1848, File No. 60-67, N.A.I.
40. *Ibid.*, W.R. Lawrence, See also *Assessment Report of Handwara Tehsil*, Jammu 1922, p. 32.
41. M.M.A. Beg, *Zara-i-Islahat* (Urdu) Srinagar, 1950, pp. 8-9. See also W. Moorcraft and G. Trebeck, *Travels in Himalayan Provinces of Hindustan and Punjab, Ladakh and Kashmir*, Vol. II, London 1971, p. 350.
42. Ganeshi Lal, *Sayahatnama* (Persian) English tr. by V.S. Suri, Chandigarh, 1976, p. 37.

In 1849 *Gagra Kotwal* and *Gulshah* were the contractors of waternuts produced in Kashmir. Their papers state that 81, 000 *kharwars* was the average produce.[43]

It was mostly procured from the Wular lake.[44] It was a big trading concern to the State. In 1856 waternuts in Srinagar were sold at the rate of one rupee a maund.[45] The state exported waternuts to *Rawalpindi* (in modern Pakistan) in exchange of rock salt during Maharaja Gulab Singh's reign (1846-57).[46] The total produce of waternuts for the year 1856-57 was 22,000 *kharwars*.[47] In 1871-72 it contributed Rs. 35,615 to the State revenues.[48] Hence it appears to have contributed a handsome amount to the State exchequer and also as a means of employment to peasants, boat-men and officials.[49]

Cotton

Cotton was grown to a small extent all over the valley. Its cultivation was carried on *karewas* and lowlying lands.

---

43. Mirza Saif-ud-Din, *Akhbarat*, Vol, II, f. 86
44. It is the largest water lake in the valley. It lies at an elevation of 5,180 ft. above the sea level and occupies an area of 12.5 sq. miles in normal condition. During floods the lake extends to one hundred sq. miles. It gives the semblances of a small sea of blue water, besides its navigational advantages for the inhabitants of adjoining areas during the period under study it produced a large quantity of waternuts. *The Jammu and Kashmir Year Book, a master document on Jammu & Kashmir the people and their life*, Jammu, 1972, p. 13.
45. Mirza, *op.cit.*, Vol. IV, f. 239.
46. *Ibid.*, See R.H. Davis, *Report on Trade and Resources of the Countries on the North Western Boundary*, Lahore, 1862, appendix XVII.
47. Mirza, *op.cit.*, Vol. X, f. 44. It was dried and then ground into flour; cakes were then made, which the richer classes made use of with salt, *ghee* and flesh. The pandits used to take it on the occasions of fast and festivals. The poor peasants simply boiled it for eating. *Gazetteer of Kashmir and Ladakh*, p. 68. Hasan, *Tarikh-i-Hassan*, Vol.I., p. 186.
48. Charles Girdlestone,*Memorandom on Kashmir*, p. 34.
49. *Ibid.*, p. 34.

Thirty six *seers* were sown per acre for the return of a produce of $1\frac{1}{2}$ *kharwars i.e.,* one hundred twenty four *seers* and eight *chhataks* per acre.[50]

Tobacco

It was cultivated in most parts of the valley. The best was grown near Srinagar town. The limited nature of its produce is borne out by the fact that annually large quantities of tobacco were imported from other countries.[51]

Hop

The hop cultivation was carried out only in Sopore. The hop garden at Dobgam Sopore was nearly 119 acres in extent, in Barzulla too 58 acres were devoted to its cultivation.[52] But till the 19th century the hop cultivation appears to have been on an experimental stage. Even as late as 1895 A.D. the total annual income from its produce was only 6000 rupees.[53]

Oil Seeds

These were largely grown in Kashmir and the principal among these oil seeds was the *rape* of which there were three varieties. The first *Tilogoglu,* was sown at the rate of six *seers* per acre and the out turn was four *kharwars.*[54] The other varieties *Sarshaf* and *Sandji* yielded a little amount of oil. Besides these large quantitites of linseed were also produced of which an average crop would be two maunds

---

50. Younghusband, *op.cit.*, p. 202.
51. Lawrence, *Valley,* p.393-394.
52. Pandit Bhag Ram, *Annual Administration Report of Jammu and Kashmir* (1889-90) Jammu, 1891, pp. 55-56.
53. Pandit Bhag Ram, *Annual Administration Report of Jammu and Kashmir State* (1894-95) Jammu, 1896, p. 105.
54. Younghusband, *op.cit.*, pp. 200-201.

per acre.[55] Rape seed provided the best oil for lighting purposes and linseed for eating. Moreover, oil was also extracted from walnuts and apricots for use in the kitchen.[56]

Saffron

The Saffron cultivation of Kashmir deserves a special mention because Kashmir was and is the only State of India where Saffron is grown. Here it was grown in two localities namely Pampore *wudar i.e. karewas* at a distance of 15 miles from Srinagar near Pampore and on a fairly limited scale in *Kishtwar*.[57] The methods of cultivation of Saffron at both the places differed from each other. In Kishtwar owing to the low rainfall and fear of Saffron being eaten up by porcupine, it was grown in flat fields, planted in rows at a depth of about eighteen inches from the surface.[58] In Kashmir valley the Saffron fields were divided into five feet square beds being surrounded by a six inches deep drainage channel and saffron was planted on these beds at a depth of four inches from surface.[59] These saffron fields remained under the crop for about ten years, during which period the number of corns was almost doubled.[60] After the Saffron cultivation for about a decade land was left lea or was ploughed for crops like and barley.[61] Ganeshi Lal says, "These fields are not watered with any stream or rivulet

55. *Ibid.*, p. 201. See also W.R. Lawrence *Assessment Report of Awantipura*, Jammu, 1920, p. 19.
56. Lawrence, *Valley*, p. 339.
    Report of British Empire Exhibition, pp. 24-25. *A note on Jammu and Kashmir State*, pp. 29-30.
57. *A Note on Jammu and Kashmir State*, p. 29-30.
58. Lawrence, *Valley*, pp. 342-43. *Report of British Empire Exhibition*, pp. 24-25.
59. Dewan Krishen Lal, *op.cit.*, Dewan Anant Ram, *Majmu-i-Report* (Urdu), 1877-78, Jammu Archives, p. 105.
60. C.E. Bates, *Gazatteer*, p. 44. Lawrence, *Valley*, p. 343.
61. *A Note on Jammu and Kashmir*, pp. 29-30.

and are dependent on the rain water alone."[62] During Maharaja Gulab Singh's time many attempts were made to extend the cultivation of Saffron but none of the soils except those of Pampore responded to the experiments of the Maharaja and his Saffron contractor Pandit Lachman Dhar.[63] In 1871 the total Saffron produce amounted to 200 *kharwars*.[64]

Relatively speaking rice was the most important crop in terms of value among food grains. The most extensive Paddy cultivation was likely to have been carried out on the lands near delta and streams which had sufficient slope to facilitate rapid drainage.[65]

Maize was mostly consumed by the poorer sections of the peasantry including the small peasants because they could not afford to take rice regularly.[67] In the first instance the peasant himself was left with very little by the state and secondly, in time of need, the peasants had to sell their rice and to subsist themselves on maize. And if at all he retained a little of rice he had to exchange it for tea, salt and clothes etc.[66] He had also to share his portion with the *pandit* and the *pir* as the case might be and with the banker, the black-smith, the barber and other village artisans.[68]

Maize was not eagerly accepted in exchange and even

62. Ganeshilal, *Sayahatnama*, p. 38.
63. Mirza, *op.cit.*, Vol. VIII., f. 28.
64. C.E. Bates, *op.cit.*, p.44. During the last two years of the decade the production declined because of the gradual decay of the bulbs. Charles Girdlestone, *Memorandom on Kashmir*, p. 39.
65. Dewan Kripa Ram, *Majmu-i-Report of Jammu and Kashmir*, (Urdu) 1873-75, Jammu Archives.
66. F. Younghusband, *Kashmir*, p. 200.
    Capt. Cunnigham *(Memo on Kashmir)*, Foreign and Sec. C, 31st March 1848, file No. 60-77, National Archives of India (N.A.I.).
67. Dewan Krishen Lal, *op.cit*.
68. There was a "good reverence" for the Brahmans and *Pirs* in the society of Kashmir of that period. It traversed through the whole social as well

(Contd. to next page)

in charity where Paddy was available but in *Kandi Illagas* (hilly areas) where maize alone was grown there was hardly any choice.[69] Apart from this, pounded maize was given as nourishment to the cattle. Thus in the agrarian economy of Kashmir, generally speaking, maize too possessed considerable significance, for it sustained a large section of the population. Though it was not commercially as important as rice, as a staple food of the peasant and the landless labourer it had a significant social role to play.[70]

Pulses were of course consumed by people now and then particularly during winter months when no leafy vegetable could be obtained.[71]

Among the fruits common in Kashmir were apple, pear, peach, cherry, apricot, almonds, walnuts and grapes. The last three varieties of fruits were of much economic value, although produced on a very limited scale.[72]

(Contd. from previous page)

as religious life of peasants in Kashmir and acquired the form of either cash offering or food. A portion of peasants produce was also handed over to artisans of village customarily comprising the above mentioned. They took a portion of the produce in lieu of their assistance offered to the peasants in the form of iron implements, pottery and so on. These artisans extracted their share irrespective of help offered to those peasants and gradually it had become a custom. Besides, these artisans claimed payments, for any service rendered, other than the customary share of produce from each peasant household. *Chief Secretariat Political and General Department file No 76 of 1896*, J.A.

69. *Ibid.*
70. The maize eating people often boiled maize like rice; they used to eat it in the form of what they called *Wat* a sort of maize jelly.
71. Pulses as an agricultural product do not appear to have been as important as they had been and still are in the Indian plains. In Kashmir, unlike in the plains, they formed no part of the regular diet, but were meant only for consumption during the scarcity of winters.
72. The almonds and walnuts are counted among dry fruits. The commanded very little or no price. Orchards had seldom any enclosure, people subsisted on fruits during famines.

Grapes

These formed an important item in the agrarian economy of Kashmir. There can be no doubt that the grape production was encouraged during Maharaja Ranbir Singh's and Maharaja Pratap Singh's time because of all the fruits it proved of great financial value to the State.[73] A large portion of produce was used for making wines. However, during Maharaja Ranbir Singh's time there was a general decline in its production which is evident from the fact that in 1870, the number of *kharwars* produced was 245, in 1877 it was 163 and in 1878 160 kharwars were produced.[74] Perhaps this could be attributed to certain natural calamities that befell the people during the period under consideration, besides political distrubances.[75] In 1889-90 Monsieur Peychand was deputed to examine the vineyards of Kashmir. He stated that the average production per 100 acres of land was 36,000 bottles of manufactured wine and the cost of cultivation per acre was Rs. 20/-.[76] In 1895 the total production used for the said purpose was 164 *kharwars*

---

73. During Maharaja Gulab Singh's time there neither existed any system of turning grapes into wine nor did Gulab Singh take any steps in this direction to make it commercial. It was during Ranbir Singh's reign for the first time that a wine manufactory was established in Srinagar and due attention was paid to the cultivation of grapes. A.L. Adams, *Wanderings of a naturalist in India*, Edinburg, 1867, p. 305.
    Dewan Anant Ram, *Majmu-i-Report*, (1877-78), pp. 96-97.
74. Dewan Anant Ram, *op.cit.*, pp. 96-97.
75. Besides the natural calamities, *i.e.* famines floods and fires and earth quakes which occurred in Kashmir in 1863, 1872, 1875, 1877, 1878 and 1879, political disturbances as a result of Shia Sunni conflicts might have also contributed to the decline in the production of grapes. Hassan, *op.cit.*, Vol. I, pp. 479-492. Ramju Dhar, *Kaifiat Intizam mulk-i-Kashmir* (Per. Ms.) (1886-87) Research Department Library, Srinagar, ff. 7-8.
76. Pandit Bhag Ram, *Annual Administration Report* (1889-90), pp. 42-43.

as is detailed below. Ten thousand four hundred thirty eight bottles were manufactured out of this produce.[77]

Apart from the food crops, cash crops and fruits Kashmir possessed an extensive and valuable forest produce comprising *Deodars, firs, blue pines, Santonian, Lac, Kuth* and other medicinal plants and flowers whose extraction provided some smount of essential oils.

Deodar

It was a valuable forest product and was found between 5000 and 9000 ft. above the sea level. The largest area occupied by this product was in *Uttar Machipora* Tehsil in *Kamraj wazarat* of Baramulla.[78] Even as late as the third decade of the 20th century very little amount of this wood had been exploited for commercial purpose. The chief obstacle in its exploitation was the absence of transport facilities and means of communication.[79]

77. The details are :

Kind of grapes	*Kharwars 1st class K.T.Seers*	*Kharwars 2nd class K.T. Seers*	*Total K. T. Seers*	*Quantity manufactured Bottles*
Black & Red	131 15 2	16 14 3	138 13 5	9,396
White	16 2 0	–	16 2 0	1,042
Total	147 17 2	16 14 3	154 15 5	10,438

Pandit Bhag Ram, *Annual Administration Report* (1885-86), Jammu, 1897, pp. 100-106.

78. A Note on Jammu and Kashmir State, p. 35.
79. *Ibid*. It is an extremely important tree of western Himalayas and of N.W. India. A tree of *Deodar* was generally of 25 ft. in girth and 200 ft. in height. See *Report of British Empire Exhibition*, pp. 16-17, Lawrence, *Valley*, pp. 78-79.

TABLE 2

The following table shows the quantity of grapes used for manufacturing different kinds of wines and the total number of bottles manufactured in Gupkar distillery from 1882-1895

GUPKAR DISTILLERY STATISTICS

					Figures in kharwars	
	Kinds of grapes used				*No. of kharwars make 100 bottles of wine*	*No. of kharwars apple make 100 bottles*
Year	*White*	*Black*	*Total*	*Apples used in*		
1882	119	60	179	4,598	1-4	
1883	173	87	260	1,781	2-0	
1884	293	147	440	61	1-13	
1885	219	109	328	-	1-13	
1886	283	142	425	-	2-11	
1887	258	412	670	-	1-15	
1888	168	33	201	-	2-10	
1889	102	26	128	-	3-11	
1890	67	41	108	100	2-8	
1891	195	118	313	-	1-8	
1892	55	30	85	422	1-8	9-15
1893	184	142	326	1,442	1-10	4-8
1894	104	95	199	2,440	1-11	4-5
1895	16	149	165	1,979	1-9	5-0
	2,336	1,491	3,827	12,623	-	-

Blue Pine

It appeared at a height of 6000 ft. and extended to 10,000 feet.[80] Its finest specimens were found in the Deodar area of forestry.[81] Trees of 15 feet in girth and 150 feet in height were not uncommon though their life is far shorter than

80. Lawrence, *Valley*, p. 80.
81. *Ibid*.

QUANTITY MANUFACTURED[82]

White wine	Red wine	Grape Brandy No. 1	Grape Brandy No. 2	Apple Brandy	Vinegar	Methy-llated spirit	Cider	Cham pane	Total No. of bottle manufactured
5,700	3,900	352	1,446	53,515	132	-	-	-	65,045
6,300	4,500	300	150	25,594	-	4,556	-	-	41,490
9,750	10,500	-	645	31,891	-	4,392	-	-	57,178
7,155	10,685	2	1,080	3,900	-	2,560	-	-	25,386
6,679	13,780	-	304	684	509	-	-	-	21,956
13,230	21,600	-	540	600	-	-	-	-	35,970
3,240	36	1,350	-	-	-	120	-	-	4,746
2,736	36	-	150	-	960	-	-	-	3,882
2,700	1,620	-	72	-	-	-	-	-	4,392
13,645	6,729	-	168	-	199	-	-	-	20,741
3,317	1,095	-	276	7,079	-	2	3,554	-	11,769
11,580	7,774	334	533	20,436	181	43	1,261	15	44,435
6,089	3,247	579	359	30,859	1,317	223	-	-	43,949
1,205	9,397	1,153	192	21,738	53	63	4,815	15	33,801
93,326	94,989	4,070	5,919	1,96,296	3,351	11,959			4,14,740

82. Ibid, pp. 134-135

that of the Deodar. It was mostly used for construction works.[83]

Silver Fir

It occupied a zone between 8000 and 11,000 feet above the sea level. Owing to its altitude it was bothersome to cut the timber. Its timber was used as a firewood by the local population on a very limited scale. In comparison to deodar and blue pine it lacked strength and fineness. The trees were generally 100 ft. long and 16 ft. in girth.[84]

Santonian

It was a very costly drug though its mother plant was most abundantly found in the forest of Kashmir. During the reign of Maharaja Pratap Singh experiments were made to extract santonian and it was established following an analysis of the plant that the collection be made sometime between July and August, when it contained a fair percentage of Santonian, that is between 4 and 9 percent.[85] It added a sum of Rs. 2.5 lakhs per annum to the State revenue.[86]

Lac

It was during the Dogra period that the existance of natural lac on black trees was noticed for the first time, but owing

---

83. Lack of transport presented a great deal of difficulty in making this tree a commercial proposition at that time wood for different uses was carried by coolies to the nearest water ways where it was floated to other areas. In some areas these logs were carried by the bullocks but the local bullock was not strong enough to carry them over long distances, the floating of wood could be done only in summer and spring months with melting of snow. *Report of British Empire Exhibition*, p. 18. See Lawrence, *Valley*, p. 80.
84. Charles Girdlestone, *op.cit.*, p. 92.
85. *A note on Jammu and Kashmir*, p. 34.
See *Report British Empire Exhibition*, pp. 18-21.
863. *Report of British Empire Exhibition*, p. 22.

to the lack of transport its exploitation on scientific lines could not be undertaken. However, during the reign of Maharaja Pratap Singh a proposal was made for the deputation of forest officer of Central Provinces for acquiring training in lac-culture.[87] Many other plants yielding medicinal drugs such as *Dizitails, Hoscymus, Bellodona, Menthol* and *Podophy* were also found and were to be paid a special attention as important commercial products.[88]

Kuth (Sanssurealappa)

It was known as Sanssurealappa; it grew extensively in Kashmir State forests and was mostly found in *Wangat* and *Sind* valleys. It was a valuable drug and was chiefly consumed in China.[89] In 1894 A.D. the income from this product was 24,000 rupees.[90] For a long time in the past the government realized only a small amount of money out of the sale of this valuable product. Later on *Kuth* market was studied and investigation were made with regard to its use. During the period of our study the price generally averaged Rs. 216 per maund.[91] In our period the revenue from this product increased from Rs. 2.5 lakhs to 14 lakhs.[92]

Apart from this, experiments were made for extraction of essential oils from wild roses, thyme and Skimmial anreola, found in the forest of Kashmir.

Notwithstanding these experiments almost to the close

---

87. *Ibid.*, pp. 21-22.
88. *A note on Jammu and Kashmir,* pp. 34-35.
89. Charles Girdlestone, *op.cit.*, p. 37. It was of four varieties, I. *Kuth,* II. *Drankhar,* III. *Poshkar* IV. *Kar*. Kashmir's population used *Kuth* as an application to ulcers, a hair wash, a medicine in cholera and also for preserving cloth against the ravages of vermin. *Gazetteer of Kashmir & Ladakh*, pp. 53.
90. Bhag Ram Pandit, *Annual Administration Report* (1894-95), Jammu, 1896, p. 141.
91. *A Note on Jammu and Kashmir*, p. 35.
92. *Ibid.*, pp. 35-36.

of 19th century the natural resources of Kashmir had not been fully exploited. The reasons for this are pretty obvious. In the first place the local demand for forest produce and mineral products was limited. There was a lack of skilled labour and the technical know-how was also absent. Over and above all these factors, geographically Kashmir was a mountain-locked country. There was a communication barrier with other parts of the country arising from the fact that transport system was little developed. As a result Kashmiri people remained unaware of the economic advancement taking place beyond these mountains.[93]

(*b*) TECHNOLOGY AND IRRIGATION

Technically agriculture within the valley was practised on traditional lines. Agricultural implements were few and simple. The ploughshare was tipped with iron and ploughing was carried out with a pair of eoxen.[94] For *Kharif* crops generally the operation of ploughing started from April just from the day of Nauroz, (the Kashmiri's new year day) and for spring crops from October to November. The rice fields were ploughed thrice or four times, wheat, barley and maize fields were ploughed twice each.[95] The whole of the plough upto the handle was made of mulberry, *Pashi,* applie or, mostly, of walnut wood. The yoke was harnessed to the neck of the animals by means of a small piece of rope and then the yoke was tied up with the beam of plough

---

93. Hassan, *op.cit.*, Vol. I, pp. 69-81.
    Lawrence, *Valley*, pp. 14-16.
94. G.T. Vigne, *Travels*, Vol. I, pp. 304-309. See illustration No. II on page 36; Dewan Kripa Ram, *Gulzar-i-Kashmir*, p. 485. J. Milne, *The road to Kashmir*, London, 1929, p. 99. Lawrence, *Valley*, pp. 305-306. Younghusband, *op.cit.*, p. 205. See also W.R. Lawrence, *Assessment Report of Mirbhari*, Jammu, 1898, pp. 26-27.

953. G.T. Vigne, *Travels*, Vol. I, pp. 304-309.

with a piece of leather (hide cord).[96] To quote Lambert "They (peasants) are very primitive in their habits. One often sees their wooden plough, being dragged by an ox and donkey. All their implements are of most inferior description.[97]

Quite a number of implements were used for preparing the soil from ploughing to sowing. Plough was the most important instrument used in cultivation of land. But the ploughshare would leave many clods unbroken. A wooden hammer was therefore used for breaking them.[98] The third stage arrived when the soil was reploughed. This time the ploughshare used was slightly smaller and its tip was of wood and not of iron.[99] After this was done the fields were watered and when water had soked the soil a little, it was supposed to be ready for the fourth or final stage of preparation of the soil for cultivation.[100] At this stage use was made of a wooden log approximately six feet long and three feet in girth. This log was yoked to a pair of oxen and it worked verily as the roller for levelling the fields and breaking any clods that might have remained in tact earlier.[101]

Use was made of wicker basket and *Kanvot*, night cap by the peasant for carrying manure.[102] In between the ploughing and harvesting time, use was often made of shovel, hoe and rake. Shovel was used for digging the

---

96. Dewan Kripa Ram, *op.cit.*, pp. 485-487. See also illustration No. II.
97. C.A. Lambert, *A Trip to Kashmir and Ladakh*, London, 1877, p. 172. From the statement of Lambert it becomes clear that the use of the donkey was also made for ploughing though not very generally.
98. See illustration No. II. fig. 1 were it is clear. It has been referred to as *yeta fur* in persian. Dewan Kripa Ram, *op.cit*, p. 485.
99. *Ibid*. p. 486.
100. *Ibid.*
101. *Ibid.*
102. *Ibid.*, p. 487. See also *A Report of British Empire Exhibition*, pp. 21-22. See illustration No. II. p. 36

Il lustration3 2

corners of the field which the plough had not reached and for embanking.[103] Hoe was used for losening the soil and for uprooting the weeds of the previous crops. Rake was used for drawing together straw and for smoothing the soil wherever necessary.[104]

The use of sickle at the time of harvesting was essential.[105] There was no special arrangement for crushing of paddy which could have saved great amount of labour. For crushing of paddy bundles of rice straw were tied against a wooden log in the presence of *Shiqdar*, the supervisor of crops, in the crushing ground and then commenced the beating of sheaves of paddy on this wooden log.[106]

For husking of paddy mortar and pestle were in general use but during the early years of Maharaja Pratap Singh's reign we have evidence that for husking of paddy there were husking machines in some areas.[107] The peasant had not to receive any special training in the use of these implements, the technique came to him through observation from early childhood.

Owing to the large amount of manure of cattle dung and abundance of wood for fuel Kashmir was very fortunately placed. Rice fields were manured and improved

---

103. Dewan Kripa Ram, *op.cit.*, p. 486.
104. *Ibid.*, page 486-487.
105. *Ibid.*, page 487.
106. Victor Jacquemont, *Letters from India*, London, 1936. pp. 219-43. Victor Jacquemont visited Kashmir during the Sikh rule. See Kripa Ram, *op.cit.*, p. 447 and the illustration No.3.
107. The State had only six husking machines called *Gindra*, worked by water. This was a large wooden axle to which in the middle two large curved wooden arms were affixed nearly opposite each other. This was being constantly worked by fall of water directed through an open pipe over a wooden wheel and these two arms in turn rose to strike to husk *Sali*. See Pratap Singh, *Diary of an Inspection Tour to Gilgit*, 1893, Jammu Archives, pp. 5-8.

by distribution of clods of fresh earth. However, it sometimes happened that all land could not be manured because of scarcity of labour.[108]

Another kind of manure was prepared by burning the standing weeds and a stubble of previous crop on peaty soils before the land was ploughed.[109] They provided potash to the soil. Besides ashes in houses were carefully stored for manuring the vegetable fields.[110]

In most parts of Kashmir crops suffered because of the non-availability of the means of minimizing the damage done to the crops by external factors. In Kashmir proper the pests like *Dada, Halov Kiri* and *Mohru* were very common.[111] The other factors which damaged the crops were *Rai* and *Handru*.[112]

Irrigation

It was a factor of prime importance because agriculture was largely dependent on it. The almost annual flooding of rivers, which was usually relied on in the exploitation of agricultural resources appears to have convinced the foreign travellers of abundance of irrigation.[113] But the

---

108. G.T. Vigne, *Travels*, Vol. I. p. 309, Lawrence, *Valley*, pp. 319-21.
109. Lawrence, *Valley*, pp. 319-21.
110. *Ibid*.
111. W.R. Lawreance, *Assessment Report of Uri Tehsil*, 1891 Jammu Archives, p. 40.
112. Handru was the name applied to that variety of paddy which failed to mature in time. It was a disease in the crop which occurred usually when there was early snowfall resulting in cold winds which prevented the ripening of grain on the plant. As a result, the grain with the husk remained by and large green. *Rai* on the contrary was the disease which ate up the main substance of grain. The husk cover of grain would ripen alright but there would be no grain in it. The disease occurred generally due to the failure of rains. *Ibid*., pp. 40-41.9
113. *Ibid*., pp. 319-321. Younghusband, *Kashmir*, pp. 222-23.

Illustration III

examination of sources leads one to conclude that the existing irrigation system presented a great hazard in carrying out normal agricultural operations. It was adequate only in a few areas. In most parts water canals could not be dug owing to difference in surface llevels.[114] And the places where water from rivers could be led on to the land, were relatively few and there could be no question of human labour for raising the water owing to the extreme intensity of labour involved. For instance the villages of *Vihu pargana* were situated at a great distance from the main water channels like *Romshi, Dood Ganga,* and much of the land was dependent on Kanchi Kul for irrigation purposes. In 1891 *Kanchi kul* was utterly broken and no arrangement was made for providing irrigation to these areas.[115] The same was the case with *ullar illaqa*. The irrigation of the area was insufficient for its agricultural requirements and the only way of increasing the water supply was by constructing tanks. This, however, could not be done due to lack of manpower and the peasants lives became more insecure.[116] Mr. Wingate who surveyed the valley for the land settlement of 1889 says, "I propose to reserve to the Durbar all rights in respect of water because in Kashmir nothing is so important or stands so much in need of control and organization. There is abundance of water but the tail villages unless very strong in men and so able to send up contingent to flight for it, cannot get it and much water runs to the waste and much irrigable land is dry.[117] After the

114. Lawrence, *Valley*, p. 323. Charles Girdlestone, *op.cit.*, p. 35. See R.G. Wrefold, *Census of India*, Vol. XXII, 1941, Jammu, 1943, p.22.

115. A.N. Raina, *Geography of Jammu & Kashmir*, pp. 69-70.

116. W.R. Lawrence, *Assessment Report of Vihu, Tehsil*, 1891, Jammu Archives, p. 12-13.

117. A. Wingate, *Preliminary Report of Land Settlement in Jammu Kashmir*, 1888, Jammu, 1889, p. 36.

commencement of the land settlement in 1888-89 the state looked after irrigation channels promptly but this was done by levying an extra irrigation cess. Secondly the development activities were concentrated in Jammu and registered very little progress in Kashmir. There was a large room for improvement. The old canal near *Ashi Mukam* if restored with improved alignment, would have irrigated the important *Karewa* of *Ranbir Singh Pora* and added largely to the state revenue. The *Hari-Khul* was for years together in a ruined condition.[118] In the year 1891-92 Rs. 6,066 were spent for repairing the irrigation works but generally improvement in the irrigation facilities in the valley started only in the fourth decade of 20th century.[119]

In fact in 1890-92 the land settlement commissioner laid down that there was much to be done in the way of agricultural improvement of the state. "In sinking irrigation wells in certain dry localities, in utilizing peat as a fuel for steam pumps, to drain the great swamps of the valley and so on. I could enumerate several kinds of agricultural improvement which would tend to benefit the state and the people. But at present I consider that these schemes are premature and that unless the land settlement is completed it is useless to take up and measure the agricultural improvement."[120]

In *Kandi illaqas* irrigation was difficult except in case of small water channels taken along the hill side.[121]

---

118. Pandit Bhag Ram, *Annual Administration Report of Jammu and Kashmir* (1895-96), Jammu, 1897, p. 117.
119. It was during the years 1931-40 that the irrigation canals like *Zaingir-Canal, Lal Khul, Martand* Canal and new canals which were fed by Jehlum *Vishav* and *Liddar* rivers were constructed. R.G. Wreford, *Census of India*, Vol. XXII, 1941, Jammu, 1943, pp. 22-23.
120. Pandit Bhag Ram, *Annual Administration Report of Jammu and Kashmir*, 1890-91, Jammu, 1892, pp. 66-67.
121. Lawrence, *Gazetteer*, p. 45, see F. Brew, *Northern Barrier of India*, pp. 172-73.

Although water was easily found from seventy to a hundred feet below the surface, wells were very few and the peasant had hardly any money to spend over sinking wells.[122] In some tracts temporary wells had been constructed to provide water to main channels. These channels were often taken over edges of *karewa* lands, which was a far more difficult process of irrigating land.[123] The well irrigation system also existed in towns like Srinagar, Anantnag, Baramulla and Sopore. It was used as a lift irrigation for vegetable lands and also in Kitchen gardens and extensive vegetable cultivation around the Dal Lake and Chattabal in Srinagar.[124]

The lift irrigation *tolsag* system was carried out by means of a long pole, to which half way down a short pole was attached to form a fork. A piece of wood joined to the upper and of the fork provided the liver for a long pole placed at right angle to it. The short end of the pole carried a large stone as a counterpoise, to the other end where hung a thick rope with an earthen bucket attached to it. The bucket was lowered into the well by pulling the rope and dragging down the pole and as the rope was released the height of the stone on the other hand raised the bucket.[125]

So far as the canal irrigation system was concerned it was also negligible and no less defective even upto the end

---

122. Capt. Knight, *Diary of a Pedestrain in Kashmir and Tibet*, London, 1863, p. 42. See Charles Girdlestone, *op.cit.*, p. 35.
123. Capt. Knight, Diary of a Pedestrain in Kashmir and Tibet, London, 1863, p. 42. See Charles Girdlestone, *op.cit.*, p. 35.
124. Mirza, *op.cit.*, Vol. VII., f. 17.
125. See illustration A petrocokino, *Kashmere three weeks in a house-boat*, London, 1920,. p. 25.
    A Petrocokino, who visited Kashmir most probably in 1917, seems to have been a very keen observer of things and provides one with certain important facts of socio-economic life in Kashmir during his sojourn there.

of 19th century. The river Jehlum also was not used for extensive irrigation within the Valley. No new canals were constructed during the period of our study. The canals newly constructed, *Nandi* and *Dandi* are attributed to Maharaja Pratap Singh which proved to be excellent sources of irrigation but actually those canals were built in the third and fourth decade of 20th century. The construction of these two canals was an extension and reconstruction of a canal built by the local peasants, the take off of which was defective and distribution inadequate.[126]

The natural resources of irrigation too were uncertain and sometimes insufficent. Capt. Knight who visited Kashmir in early 1862 observes "No rain having fallen as yet, the springs and rivers were all dry."[127] The chief danger arose from the excessive rains with floods in alluvial pleatueax injured by prolonged moisture and early snow and uncertain rainfall.[128] In 1854 the rains cause the flood and destroyed the whole harvest in lowlying areas.[129] In 1855 when the harvest had not been collected the valley witnessed early snowfall.[130]

Hassan says, "During Samvat 1934 and Hijra 1294 *i.e.* 1877 A.D. in the month of Katak (*i.e.* September/October) when Maharaja Ranbir Singh was ill and administration was in the hands of Wazir Punoo it rained continuously for two and a half months. The river Jehlum was in spate and the Wular lake too was flooded; consequently the crop of

---

126. Wreford, *Census*, 1941, p. 23. These canals irrigated lands between Jehlum and its tributaries, the *Vishva* river, *Liddar, Ranbiara, Sandran* and *Brangi*.
M.A. Stein, *Ancient Geography of Kashmir*, pp. 99-102.
127. A. Neve, *Thirty Years in Kashmir*, London, 1913, p. 30.
128. Mirza, *op.cit.*, Vol.I, ff. 52-53.
129. *Ibid.*, Vol. V, f 42. See also Ramju Dhar, *Kaifiat-Itizam-Mulk-i-Kashmir* (Presian Ms.) Research Department Library, Srinagar, f. 9.
130. *Ibid.*, Vol. VIII, f. 128.

rice was destroyed. The administration did not give thought of impending famine. However, Wazir Punoo issued two lakh *kharwars of Shali* from reserved stock with a view to putting off this symptomatic appearance of famine till the next spring."[131] In 1896 heavy snow fall prevented the usual area of land being brought under cultivation, which was followed by heavy rains and the peasant's condition deteriorated to a greater extent. The State did not fail to collect the irrigation cess even though ever since 1880 when a cash assessment had been made, the peasants had to attend to irrigation themselves.[132]

Some areas depended on spring water for irrigation but this spring water was very cold and took much time to reach a certain degree of temperature necessary for rice cultivation. Secondly it did not carry fertility of silt with it. On the other hand "spring water bears scum which is considered bad for rice."[133]

---

131. Hasan, *op.cit.*, Vol, I, pp. 464-65.

در زمان ایالت رنبیر سنگه و انتظام وزیر پنون در سنه ۱۲۹۳ هـ سمت ۱۹۳۲ بکرمی
در ماه کتک که فصل شالی در صحرا درو طلب بود باران مسلسل بار از آسمان باریدن
گرفت که تا عرصهٔ دو نیم ماه متواتر و مستدام بود - دریای بهت طغیانی گشت و تا اول
برف سپیدی شد و فصل شالی با خاک آمیخت آنچه به درو رسیده بود در خرمن ها
بوسیده گشت ناظم را خیال قحط به خاطر نرفت و ذخایر موجودی دو لک خروار
در کار سازی از دست داد تا ایام بهار آثار قحط ظاهر نشد -

132 Pandit Bhag Ram, *Annual Administration Report of Jammu and Kashmir*, Jammu, 1893, pp. 66-67.

133 Lawrence, *Gazetteer*, p. 45.

3
Land Revenue System

Methods of Assessment

The land revenue system was extremely ill-organized at the time Maharaja Gulab Singh acquired Kashmir in 1846 A.D.[1] Revenue officials were acting in an arbitrary manner with regard to the assessment and collection of land revenue.

During the Mughal period (1586-1753) the method of assessment prevalent in Kashmir was crop-sharing under *Nasq*. Irfan Habib very rightly remarks that *Nasq* system of assessment in Kashmir was "Subordinate to crop sharing."[2]

---

1. On conclusion of the second Anglo-Sikh war, which took place several years after the death of Maharaja Ranjit Singh, Gulab Singh played an effective role in bringing about the treaty between the British and the Sikhs. For his services Gulab Singh received Kashmir from British under the treaty of Amritsar in March 1846.
   H.M. Lawrence, *Transfer of Govt. to Maharaja Gulab Singh*, Section C, 28th January 1848, file Nos. 33-44, Jammu Archives.
   Dewan Kripa Ram, *Gulab-nama*, English tr. by S.S. Chark Delhi, 1977, pp. 290-315.
   A.P. Nicholson *Scrapes of paper, India's broken treaties, her princes and her problem*, London, 1930, pp. 88-90. See also S.M. Latif, *History of Punjab*, Delhi 1964, pp. 440-454.
   K.M. Panikar, *Gulab Singh, the founder of Jammu & Kashmir State*, London, 1930, pp. 104-105.
2. Irfan Habib, *Agrarian System of Mughal India*, Bombay, 1963, pp. 215-216.
   Kripa Ram, *Majmu-i-Report* (1872-73) (Urdu), pp. 17-18.

Under Afghan rule (1753-1819) the revenue system of Kashmir did not alter significantly except for the introduction of some new *Abwabs* which were levied on the peasants in addition to the usual land revenue demand.[3]

The Sikh rulers (1819-1846) also allowed the system of crop sharing as the method of assessment in Kashmir.[4]

Crop sharing at the best of times leaves considerable loopholes for corruption. In times of uncertainty, when the hand of government control over its officials grows feeble, the officials' arbitrary demands tend to soar.

During Maharaja Gulab Singh's reign at the very outset, all matters involving the general administration, the land revenue system and the internal and external trade were submitted to him for his consideration but he did not propose any structural change in the revenue administration. He appears to have more or less adhered to the Sikh system.[5]

The method of assessment during Maharaja Gulab

---

3. Ramju Dhar, *Kaifiyat Intizam-i-mulk-i-Kashmir*, (Per. Ms.) Research Department Library, Srinagar, ff. 2-3. Dewan Kripa Ram, *Gulzar-i-Kashmir*, pp. 256-57.
   Dewan Kripa Ram, *Majmu-i-Report* (1872-73) Urdu, pp. 17-18. Dewan Anant Ram, *Report Majmu-i Jammu-va-Kashmir and Tibet*, (1873-75) (Urdu) Jammu Archives, pp. 32-33.
4. H.M. Lawrence, *Transfer of Govt. to Maharaja Gulab Singh* Section C, 28th January, 1848, file Nos. 33-44, Jammu Archives. *Diary of P.S Melvill Punjab Government Records*, Lahore, 1911-15, Vol.VI. pp. 191-197, 217.
   Dewan Krishan Lal, *Account of Kashmir Foreign and Sec.* 31 March, 1848, No. 68. N.A.I.
   Ramju Dhar, *op.cit.*, ff. 4-6
   Indu Banga, *Agrarian System of the Sikhs*, Delhi 1978, p. 88, n.2.
5. Mirza Saif-ud-Din, *Akhbarat*, Vol. I. ff. 1-4.
   H.M. Lawrence, *op.cit.*, Section C, 28th January, 1848 file Nos. 33-44, Jammu Archives.
   John Lawrence, *Condition of Kashmir Secret Committee* 31 March, 1848 No. 66-77, N.A.I. Kripa Ram, *Majmu-i-Report* (1872-73), p. 18.
   A. Wingate, *op.cit.*, p. 54.

Singh's time was a peculiar system of *Batai.*[6] Under this system the estimate of production was made when the grain was in heafs and was divided in the heaps after threashing as in regular *Batai.*[7] The crop was harvested by the peasants and collected in stocks *(gunnies)* consisting of a certain number of *kharwars.*[8]

After the amount of each man's produce was determined by the *kardar* with the help of the *Shiqdar*, the government demand was ascertained. The state demand at the time consisted of one haly of the produce. In addition to this the peasant had to pay about sixteen per cent of the produce as *Trakee* and *Abwabs.*[9] The total demand amounted

---

6. H.M. Lawrence, *op.cit.*, Section C, 28th January 1848, file Nos. 33-44, Jammu Archives.
   Nicholson's letter containing information of Kashmir Foreign and Sec.C. Dec. 1846. No. 1266, N.A.I. See also R.K. Parmu, *History of Dogra rule in Kashmir*, typed Ms. p. 29-31. Dr. Parmu (Director, History Unit, Jammu and Kashmir) was kind enough to permit me to go through his manuscript of Dogra history before sending it to press.
7. Because in *Batai* system the division of grains was made on threshing floors. The other two methods of *Batai* were *Khet Batai* and *Lang Batai* under the former a certain measured area of standing crop was taken the produce of which was assumed to represent the share of the entire holding. Under the *Lang Batai* system the peasant divided the grain into as many heaps as there were shares and that revenue official took the heap that he liked. Badan Powell, *Land System of British India*, Delhi 1967, 3 Vols. Vol. I, pp. 274-75. But the system of *Batai* applied to Kashmir apears dissimilar from these systems of *Batai*.
8. H.M.Lawrence, *op.cit*, Section C, 28th January, 1848, file Nos. 33-34, Jammu Archives.
9. The term *trakee* meant a tax. Under this system when all was said and done about the collection of revenue, a *trak* of paddy (of 5 seers of 83 chhataks) was charged from peasants per *kharwar*. This tax was introduced in Kashmir by Afghan rulers. *Abwabs* were the other cesses levied by various revenue officials. Kripa Ram, *Gulzar-i-Kashmir*, pp. 256-57.
   Ramju Dhar, *op.cit.*, ff. 2-3.
   See also *Diary of R.G.Taylor*, Punjab Government Records (1847-49), Vol. VI., p. 80.

to ⅔ of the produce and ⅓ was left to the peasant.[10] Under this particular system then in vogue, the state took a certain number of *kharwars* in kind and the rest in *Mobiyah.*[11] *Mobiyah* was a system by which the government was entitled to convert a certain number of traks in every kharwar into money at one or more established market rates. We cite the example of Sat Ram, a peasant of Pargana *Adwin* of Kashmir to illustrate the system.

Hardohissa (total produce)	... 90 *kharwars*
Sarkaree Hissa (Govt. share)	... 45 *kharwars*
Trakee and *Abwabs*	... 15 *kharwars*
The total Govt. demand	... 60 *kharwars*

Now out of this share the state took in *Mobiyah* at various rates 37 *kharwars* and 8 *traks* and remaining twenty two *kharwars* and eight *traks* in kind. The allowance to be deducted for carriage was two *kharwars* and six *traks* and there remained twenty *kharwars* and two *traks.*[12]

Thus in another case 62.5 per cent of the state share of revenue was commuted into cash on the basis of price prescribed by the state and 37.5 per cent of the produce was collected in kind.[13]

Out of 37 *kharwars* and 8 *traks* commuted into cash, 22 *kharwars* and 8 *traks* were converted into money at the rate of 1.37 per *kharwar* and the remaining 15 *kharwars* at the rate of 1.25 per *kharwar.*[14]

But this system of assessment was applied to the *sarkasht*

---

10. H.M. Lawrence, *op.cit.*, Capt. Cunnigham's Memo, *Foreign Deptt.* See. c. 31 March, 1848, No. 66-77.
11. H.M. Lawrence, *op.cit.*, Section C, 28th January, 1848, File Nos. 33-44, Jammu Archives.
12. H.M. Lawrence, *op.cit.*
13. *Ibid.*, The market rates were determined by the State.
14. *Ibid.*

land. However, on *Paikasht* and *Navabadee* lands the rates of assessment were slightly less.[15] Both *rabi* and *kharif* crops were assessed in the same manner. No separate method was adopted for cash crops like cotton, tobacco, oilseeds etc.[16]

This form of *Batai* remained the most important and widely applied method of assessment in Kashmir. However, certain other methods of assessment were also experimented with from time to time. The *Akhbarat* of Mirza Saf-ud-Din furnishes us with a detailed information on different methods of assessment tried at various stages.[17] Mirza Saif-ud-Din says that the revenue officials were engaged day and night to prepare a register of assessment in 1846.[18] In that year Devi Dutta, a Punjabi land revenue expert was directed by Maharaja Gulab Singh to find out ways and means to increase the assessment as much as possible.[19] Unfortunately the records do not mention the exact nature of the method of assessment worked out by Devi Dutta of Punjab. All that is known that he assessed the lands according to *kanals* and the revenue was to be collected from town to town and from village to village at the uniform rate of rupees two a *kanal* and a *kharwar* of land was to be assessed at the rate of 120 rupees.[20]

Again in the winter of 1848 Maharaja Gulab Singh deputed Moulvi Mazhar Ali and Dewan Kanahya to assess

---

15. There were two broad divisions of land in Kashmir *sarkasht* and *paikasht*. Those lands which were under regular cultivation near the city were called *sarkasht* lands. The lands which were cultivated by the peasants living in other villages were known as *paikasht*. *Ibid*. See also R.K. Parmu, *History of Dogra Rule in Kashmir*, Ms. p. 31.
16. *Ibid.*, The *Navabadee* lands were those which were newly brought under cultivation.
17. Mirza Saif-ud-Din, *Akhbarat*, Vol. I., f. 45.
18. *Ibid.*, Vol. II., f. 87.
19. *Ibid.*, Vol. II., ff. 87-88.
20. *Ibid.*, Vol. II., ff. 3 and 46.

the produce of Paddy in Pargana *Ich-Nagam.*[21]

In 1851 Maharaja Gulab Singh's officials completed the assessment operations in Handwara Tehsils and fixed in every two *kharwars* of produce of ½ *traks* as the share of the cultivator and one *kharwar* and five *traks* as the share of the state and the remaining one *trak* was to meet the demands of the secretariat staff and contingencies. Under this system of assessment the share of the peasant was further reduced to only 29.5 per cent of the total produce.[22]

In 1852 for administrative purposes Maharaja Gulab Singh got the whole of the valley divided into seven divisions and tried to follow the British code but owing to the incompetent and illiterate Kashmir revenue staff this could not succeed.[23]

In 1853 some relaxation was made in the assessment of waste lands which had been brought under cultivation. It was laid down that the state shall take two parts out of the five of the produce of these lands the other three parts will be left to the peasant.[24] In 1854 the work of assessment and collection was entrusted to military commanding officers.[25]

Notwithstanding these experiments the method of assessment prevalent for most of the time in Kashmir during the reign of Maharaja Gulab Singh remained *Batai*

---

21 *Ibid.*

22. *Ibid.*, Vol. V., ff. 60-62.

23. *Ibid.*, ff.60-62. It was in 1846 that the greater part of Punjab came under British land revenue administration. Summary settlements were made and regular settlements commenced. Baden Powell, *Land Systems of British India*, pp. 532-34. The immediate relief that the regular settlements provided to the people of Punjab appear to have convinced Gulab Singh of the necessity of introducing the British code.

24. F. Younghusband, *Kashmir*, pp. 173-74.

25. The assigning of the work of assessment and collection to military commanding officers must have taken place most probably because large amount of revenue was in arrears. See Mirza, *op.cit.*, VCL.IV, f. 114, also Vol. VIII., ff. 8,62.

which he inherited from the Sikh regime. Mr. A. Wingate who made preliminary arrangements for the land settlement in Kashmir says that during Maharaja Gulab Singh's time Sikh procedure was followed and the same is borne out by G.R. Taylor who visited Kashmir during Maharaja Gulab Singh's period.[26]

During Maharaja Gulab Singh's time several attempts were made to introduce a satisfactory method of assessment but all of them proved unsatisfactory and also lacked a definite purpose.[27]

In 1857 Maharaja Ranbir Singh took over the administration of Kashmir. He annually farmed out the circles of villages to contractors called *Kardars.*[28] In 1859 the valley of Kashmir was divided by these *kardars* into several fiscal units for the purpose of assessment and each unit of land under their charge was further subdivided into three parts. In the two lower parts rice was allowed to be grown, and in the third part no rice cultivation was allowed.[29] Expectedly every *kardar* was bent upon collecting as much as he could. Thus the *kardar* dictated not only the method of assessment of his choice to the peasants but also the crop to be sown by them.

---

26. A Wingate, *op.cit.*, 54-55. *Diary of G.R. Taylor*, Punjab Govt. Records (1847-49), p. 24-25.
27. The failure of these attempts can most probably be attributed to the arbitrariness followed by the revenue staff which met their timely needs. *Diary of G.R. Taylor*, Punjab Govt. Records (1847-49) Vol. VI., p. 24-25.
28. A. Wingate, *op.cit.*, pp. 54-60. Ramju Dhar, *op.cit.*, ff. 8-9.
29. The third part was generally that portion of land which was on high altitude so the *kardars* did not permit rice cultivation because it could prove a failure. Lawrence, Valley, p. 402.
    See Dewan Anant Ram, *Majmu-i-Report of Jammu Kashmir and Tibet*, (1873-75), pp. 30-34.
    P.N.K. Bamzai, *History of Kashmir, Political, Social and Cultural*, Delhi, 1962, p. 688.

In 1860 the *pargana* divisions of Kashmir were liquidated and they were merged into *chakladari* system. The *chakla* was usually large than the *pargana* and its revenue was formed out to *chakladars.* In this *chakladari* system of assessment, the average collections of five years prior to *chakladari* system were taken as the base. This system of assessment was first introduced for three years; later on 1863 at the completion of the first term the assessment was renewed. Some slight enhancement in revenues took place at this time. Unfortunately the natural calamities that took place during the years 1864-65; the assessment therefore could not be carried out. Again from 1867 the system worked for some time by demanding one half from *Rabi* crops and sixty per cent from the *Kharif* harvest as the state share. This system was seriously opposed by the people from *Vihu ,Nagam* and *Shopian parganas* and finally the system died down because the peasants were not ready to carry on with the system of lease for quite some time.[30]

However, by 1869 the practice of contracting with *Muqadams* or the peasants gradually established itself in place of farming out of lands to the *kardars.*[31] In 1873 Maharaja Ranbir Singh got the village contracts divided into *assamiwar khewats. Khewat* or village cash assessment was made and the state share was taken either in cash or in kind from each man.[32] In 1876 fresh contracts were made

---

30. H.L.P. Wynne, *Report on Kashmir,* 1872, For Pol. A, file Nos. 343-349. January 1873, NAI.
31. A. Wingate, *op.cit.,* pp. 54-55.
32. *Ibid.,* Dr. R.K. Parmu without any evidence states that in 1870 Maharaja Ranbir Singh introduced a settlement department on the Punjab pattern. But this fact is not borne out by any of the Persian or English records of the time. Even Mr. Wingate who presented the preliminary report for carrying out elaborate land settlement does not corroborate this statement of Dr. Parmu. See his *History of Dogra rule in Kashmir,* Ms., p. 85.

either with *Muqadams* or *kardars* or peasants and two *traks* per kharwar were added to the previous assessment.[33] In 1877, due to famine, new contracts could not be carried out and the state share was collected in kind only. This system lasted upto 1880 when a new *assamiwar khewat* or village cash assessment was made which was based upon the previous years' collections.[34] These were estimated in cash but the amount was payable in cash or in kind as it suited to the peasant.[35] This method of *assamiwar khewat* was arrived at by taking the collections of two years *i.e.* 1877 and 1878 A.D. and the average was struck. Then gross produce was recorded and one half was taken as the government share; to this 25 per cent were added as *Trakee*.[36] The quantity obtained thus in these *kharwars* was commuted into money at standard prices which were used for commutation.[37]

In 1882 another method of assessment known as *Izadboli* or auctioning of the villages was introduced.[38] Under this system the *mustajir* or bidder paid lumpsum to the state and then exacted as much as he could from a village without taking into consideration the condition of crop. Some times the *mustajir's* absconded without making payment to the state. As a result it was immediately

---

33. *Ibid.*
34. Dewan Kripa Ram, *Majum-i-Report*, pp. 21-23. Lawrence, *Valley*, pp. 402-405.
35. A. Wingate, *op.cit.*, pp. 54-55.
36. The collection was made on the *kharwar* of 16 *traks* and after that the whole quantity was converted into 15 *trak kharwars*. The 15 trak *kharwar* was called *kachha kharwar* and was used for all crops which included cotton, oilseeds, saffron and other crops, if any.
 Ibid., pp. 54-55.
37. *Ibid.*
38. W.R. Lawrence, *Report on the position of cultivating classes in Kashmir*, Foreign Deptt. Sec. E.Feb. 1890. NAI. See also Lawrence, *Valley*, p. 408. Bamzai, *op.cit.*, p. 689.

TABLE 3

The following table shows how the assamiwar khewat was arrived at by taking one village as a sample.[39]

Crop	*Gross produce 16 trak kharwars*			*State share after adding trakee*			*Govt. share calculated in rupees*		
	kh.	*tr.*	*ch.*	*kh.*	*tr.*	*ch.*	*Rs.*	*a.*	*pies.*
Serson	0	6	0	0	3	0	1	8	0
Oil seed	4	13	0	2	6	2	21	11	6
Cotton	3	0	1½	1	8	2	21	3	3
Mong	1	5	1	0	12	1½	6	1	9
Paddy	1438	0	0	897	1	0	1844	2	0

discontinued after registering huge loss to the state revenues and *khewat* system was resumed.[40]

Under *khewat* system each Tehsildar was informed of the amount he was expected to contribute to the total. He converted this quantity into cash on the basis of rupees two per *kharwar* and out of every one rupee 10 annas were fixed as his share.[41] Then he would give instruction for the collection of so many *kharwars* from each village and the total collections came to the amount which was fixed at head quarters or sometimes more than that.

However, the *khewat* system of assessment was no more oppressive than the *Batai*. In the *khewat* system the peasant was certain to retain at least a small portion of the produce. But there was constant opposition to the *khewat* system of

39. A. Wingate, *op.cit.*, pp. 54-55.
From the given table it becomes clear that the rates of assessment varried from crop to crop. In Sarson the rate, including *trakee*, is one-half; in paddy it is more than one-half.
40. *Ibid.*, See Dewan Kripa Ram, *Majmu-i-Report of Jammu-va-Kashmir and Tibet*, pp. 21-23.
41. Lawrence, *Report on the position of cultivating classes in Kashmir.* Foreign Deptt. Sec. E. Feb. 1890, N.A.I.

assessment from revenue officials who preferred the collection of revenue in kind,[42] because the *khewat* system reduced their share in produce. While as in *Batai* they were able to collect in pre-requisites more than what they had been getting under *khewat*..[43] The *Batai* system also provided them with the opportunity to appoint subordinate staff, *i.e.* the watchman, the weighman etc.[44] who could help them in all the fraudulent practices.

In 1885 Maharaja Pratap Singh came to the throne and soon after his accession a land settlement was commenced. Since 1869 Maharaja Ranbir Singh had been negotiating with the British government for the services of two I.C.S. land experts. It was on 15th of January, 1887, that Mr. A. Wingate joined as the settlement officer of Kashmir for carrying out a detailed land settlement.[45] Mr. Wingate made preliminary arrangements for the land-settlement in 1887 but it was not until 1889 that a regular land settlement commenced. The work which had been entrusted to Mr. A. Wingate was taken over by W.R. Lawrence. A settlement Department was established. A code of rules and forms (Athavatri) given to the peasant

---

42. The influential *lambardars* and other revenue officials who stood between the state and the peasant tried their best to prevent any permanent settlement because it went against their interests. Even the officials like Dewan Lachman Dass, Dewan of Kashmir province, himself a big landlord of the state, wanted the crop settlement to continue. See *Petition of Dewan Lachman Dass against the cash settlement, Chief Secretariate Pol. and Gen. Deptt. file No. 2 of 1896*, Jammu Archives.
43. *Ibid.* See also a Wingate, *op.cit.*, pp. 55-56.
44. *Petition of Dewan gachman Dass against the Cash Settlement, Chief Sec. op.ct.*, for details see Lawrence, *Valley*, pp. 404-430.
45. *Foreign Deptt. See, E. October 1886, file No. 235-300* N.A.I. S.R. Temple, *India in 1880*, London, 1881, pp. 213-15, Lawrence, *Valley*, p. 407. A.P. Nicholson, *Scrapes of paper, India's broken treaties her princes her problem*,pp. 96-109. Younghusband, *op.cit.*, pp. 190-193.

for settlement purposes were prepared. A system for accounts was arranged and details for the subordinate staff to be locally entertained were decided upon with the help of Colonel Wace, then financial commissioner of the Punjab and later Narsing Dass who was appointed as Assistant Settlement Officer.[46]

Mr. Lawrence after careful examination of the situation and after looking into the previous methods of assessment was in favour of assessing the land revenue demand in cash only but under various pulls and pressures he had to agree to a settlement where by the land revenue was made payable both in cash and kind.[47]

In the initial stages Lawrence also had to surmount many difficulties in introducing this kind of land settlement. In one of the assessment reports he says, "It is my duty to purpose such an assessment as can be paid and as a rule in fixing the assessment I take into consideration the amount which has been paid by the village on account of *Girftani i.e.* arrears. If Tehsildars are allowed to collect the *Girftani* in addition to the proposed revenue then they will again get opportunities of peculation, the work done by the settlement will become useless and the State revenue will again fell into hopeless confusion. I should remark here that several villages were not ready to accept the new assessment. They preferred the old ficticious system, so that they may be regarded as broken villages *i.e. Skim-ul-Hal* because with the consultations of Tehsil officials large suspension of revenue was made annually. As a result the officials pocketed half

---

46. Pandit Bhag Ram, *Administration Report of Jammu and Kashmir State* (1889-90) Jammu, 1891, pp. 22-23.
47. *Ibid.*, Lawrence, *Valley*, p.407.
See *Petition of Dewan Lachman Dass, against the cash Settlement 1896, op.cit.*

the amount thus suspended. So I had to face much difficulty in getting the new assessment accepted."[48]

Lawrence took pains to convince the peasants that the new assessment was fair and nothing beyond the amount assessed was to be taken from them. Lawrence states in his settlement records that the revenue of these areas, which had been assigned by the state to individuals as *jagir*, was not subject to the settlement establishment for the new methods of assessment. So far as the *Muafi* lands were concerned they were looked after by the *Darmarth* department.[49]

According to the new land settlement the assessment was fixed for 14 years and due thought was given to all the problems that the peasant had to face in carrying out cultivation. The basis of the assessment was that the net produce of each village was estimated taking into account the crops grown in different villages.[50]

---

48. W.R. Lawrence, *Assessment Report of Ich-Nagam Tehsil of Kashmir*, Jammu, 1891, pp. 7-9.
49. *Ibid.*, The records do not mention whether it was state or the *jagirdars* who denied access to these records of *jagir* holdings and did not permit Lawrence to impose the new assessment on them. Secondly since the *Muafi* lands were dealt with by the *Darmarth* Department they should have dealt with those *muafis* only which had been granted to the Hindus and their religious institutions. It is not clear who looked after the Muslim *Muafi* lands. However, *muafi* lands continued in possession of *Muafidars* even upto present and there is a good number of *Pattas* in some of the Brahmin and Sayyid families substantiating this fact.
50. The main features of the settlement introduced by Lawrence were:-
    - I. The state demand was fixed for 14 years.
    - II. Payment in cash was substituted for payment in kind (But records show that payment in kind continued for sometime.)
    - III. Use of force in collecting the revenue was abolished.
    - IV. Begar was to be abolished gradually.
    - V. Occupancy rights were conferred on cultivators in undisputed lands.

(Contd. to Next Page)

Land Revenue Demand

The land revenue demand from the days of the Mughals upto 1887, when the regular land settlement commenced, was to a large extent fickle and arbitrary. During the Mughal period after the conquest of Kashmir Akbar ordered that one half should be demanded but the revenue collectors charged at times as much as two thirds.[51]

Under the Afghans the state demand on the main cereal was very high. They charged five eights of rice, though all vegetables and other minor cereals remained untaxed.[52]

The Sikh rulers of Kashmir fixed the State's share of produce generally at one half but over and above this demand the state also levied certain cesses such as *Mandri, Tambul, Rasum-i-Doftar* and *Nazrana*.[53] In addition to these,

---

(Contd. from previous page)

VI. Permanent but non-hereditary rights were granted to those who accepted the first assessment.

VII. All land was valued on the basis of produce previous collection and irrigation.

VIII. *Rasum* and other exactions were abolished.

IX. Rents and liabilities of cultivators were defined.

X. The State share of the revenue was fixed at 30 per cent of gross produce.

D.K. Palit, *Jammu and Kashmir Arms*, p. 91.

51. Irfan Habib *Agrarian System*, pp. 192-93.
52. The State demand worked to 60 to 65 per cent. Kripa Ram, *Majmu-i-Report* (1872-73) pp. 17-18.
Kripa Ram, *Gulzar-i-Kashmir*, pp. 256-57.
See also *Gazetteer of Kashmir and Ladakh*, p. 105.
53. *Mandri* meant a share for temples and other religious endowments; *Tambul* marriage levy. *Rasum-i-Doftar* was a share from the peasants for clerical staff of revenue department. It is not certain whether or not the *numbardar* or village headman actually distributed the whole amount among clerks. *Nazrana* was levied four times a year on festive occasions.

H.M. Lawrence, *op.cit.*, Diary of R.G.Taylor, Punjab Govt. Records (1847-49) VII., p. 24-25. See also *Gazetteer of Kashmir and Ladakh*, p. 105.

the *trakee* system of the Afghans was continued by the Sikhs. The Sikhs charged four *traks* per *kharwar* of paddy from the peasants.[54] Only *pirs* and *pandits* paid this cess at the rate of two *traks* per *kharwar*.[55] An addition of Rs. 1-9-0 per cent was charged by the state.[56]

Cesses were also levied on cash and *kimiti* crop as well as on sheep and goats.[57] These cesses charged over and above the land revenue raised the demand to such an extent as to leave very little with the peasant.

The total burden of taxes levied on the peasant amounted to 60 per cent of the gross produce.[58]

Under Governor Mian Singh who was considerate enough to abolish many cesses, the State share of produce was fixed at a half of the produce. However, the same rate was demanded on pulses, tobacco, cotton and red pepper.[59] Shaikh Ghulam Mohi-ud-Din, the last Governor of Kashmir under the Sikhs retained the same system except that he provided a remission of two traks to the peasant of *Sir Kasht*

---

54. A. Wingate, *op.cit.*, p. 54. H.M. Lawrence, *op.cit.*, *Gazetteer of Kashmir and Ladakh*, p. 105.
55. Hassan, *op.cit.*, Vol.II., p. 657. *Gazetteer of Kashmir and Ladakh*, p. 105. Here it appears that Sikhs did not dispense with the system they had inherited from the Afghans.
56. Besides this half a *trak* was charged per *kharwar*, which was shared by *Patwari and Qanongo*. Mir Ahmad, *Dastural-Amal-i-Kashmir*, Ms. M.829, Punjab State Archives Patiala, Part II, f. 59.
57. The cash crops included cotton, tobacco, saffron, while the *kimiti* crops were oilseeds, honey, fruits like almonds and walnuts. Ganeshi Lal, *Sayahatnama*, pp. 37-38.
Diary of R.G. Iaylor (1847-49), Punjab Govt. Records, Vol. VI., pp. 24-26.
58. *Gazetteer of Kashmir and Ladakh*, p. 105.
59. He also levied *trakee* at the rate of five *traks* though he later reduced it to four *traks* per *kharwar*. H.M. Lawrence, *op.cit.*, Kripa Ram, *Gulzar-i-Kashmir*, pp. 256-57. See also Dewan Amarnath, *Zafarnama-i-Ranjit Singh* (per). ed. by Sita Ram Kohili, Lahore, 1928, pp. 226-27. Lawrence, *Valley*, p. 200. *Tarikh-i-Kalan*, ff. 204-06.

lands on the condition that they shall increase the area under cultivation.[60]

The magnitude of land revenue demand was little less severe under Maharaja Gulab Singh than it was under the Afghans and the Sikhs.[61] The State under Gulab Singh realized the land revenue in kind, theoretically at the rate of one half of the produce. Maharaja Gulab Singh reduced the rate of *trakee* on *Sirkasht* lands of the whole country to three *traks.* However, no concession was made on Paikasht lands and the *trakee* was levied at the rate of two *traks* as before.[62] Besides Maharaja Gulab Singh reduced the rate on cotton from Rs. 10 to Rs. 7.[63]

But this was hardly the end of exactions. Under Maharaja Gulab Singh the state collected levies such as *Kharch* and *Abwab,* like *Rasudat,*[64] *Tilsiah Chahar Magz,*[65] *Rusud-i-Khah,*[66] *Sur-i-dehee,*[67] *Dawga-i-Daftar,*[68] *Rusud*

---

60. S.N. Koul, *Kashmir Economics*, p. 58.
61. Though the Sikh procedure was followed in general but some slight relaxation were made in favour of lands newly cultivated. A few large areas of land were lying waste. It seems that under Maharaja Gulab Singh much of the waste lands was reclaimed. A. Wingate, *op.cit.*, p. 54.
62. Mirza, *op.cit.*, Vol. I, f. 26, H.M. Lawrence, *op.cit.*
63. H.M. Lawrence *op.cit.*, See also S.K.Koul, *Kashmir Economics*, pp. 58-59.
64. It was a tax on fruit trees, willows and vegetables according to the quantity produced. Generally it varied from 10 to 100 rupees per village. H.M. Lawrence, *Transfer of Govt. to Maharaja Gulab Singh*, 28 June, 1848.
65. It was a separate tax on walnut trees. One rupee was charged for 2500 walnuts, *Ibid.*
66. This cess was levied on straw at the rate of one anna per hundred *kharwars, Ibid.*
67. It was charged at the rate of one rupee for all small and big villages, *Ibid.* (The purpose is not known).
68. This cess amounted to Rs. 150 on the whole country, *Ibid.* (purpose not known).

Shumag-Khulbul,[69] *Sur-i-Sudhee-Jinsi,*[70] *Chungee,*[71] *Thandari,*[72] *Musad-ah,*[73] *Khushraza,*[74] *Boodkee,*[75] *Sur-Sudhee-Nukdee,*[76] Munwa-tee,[77] *Neem Manwattee Harkaree*[78] *Shiqdaree,*[79] . *Sazowul,*[80] *Tehvildaree,*[81] *Khidmatgaree,*[82] *Kardaree,*[83]

---

69. It was levied at the rate of 2 rupees per hundred *kharwars* of rice, *Ibid.*, (purpose to known).
70. This was charged at one *kharwar* per 100 *kharwars Ibid.* (purpose not known).
71. It was deducted on account of toll at the rate of 4 *traks* per 100 *kharwars, Ibid.*
72. The state used to levy 41/2 *seers* in every *kharwar* to meet the expenses of *Hanjis* (boatment) as a hire for transporting the collected revenue from villages to the city, *Ibid.*
73. This cess was levied on account of seed provided by the state to the peasants. The state did not advance the seed to the peasants regularly but taxed them regularly. This cess was shared by the state with *Kardar* who would get one *seer* out of two *traks* levied per *kharwar*. *Ibid.*
74. It was known as a tax of one's own choice for keeping revenue officials obliged and kind; (which they never were) and was charged at the rate of two rupees per head, Mirza Saif-ud-Din, *Akhbarat*, Vol. I, ff. 22-23.
75. The purpose of this cess is not known but it was charged at the rate of two *traks* per *kharwar*. H.M.Lawrence, *op.cit.*
76. It was levied at the rate of one rupee and nine annas per hundred *kharwars, Ibid.* (purpose unknown)
77. It was levied and the rate of 1½ *seers* per *kharwar. Ibid.*
78. This cess was realized for meeting the expenses of *Harkar* (the state spy appointed for looking after the crops).. This cess amounted to one *seer* per *kharwar, Ibid.* See also Ramju Dhar, *op.cit.*, f. 3b. (Persian ms.)
79. On account of *Shiqdars* expenses (the watchman of crops) two *seers* were deducted per *kharwar* of paddy, *Ibid.*
80. This tax was collected at the rate of about two *seers* per *kharwar* of paddy for *Sazawul,* another revenue official, *Ibid.*
81. The term *Tehvildaree* meant a tax levied for the *Tehvildar* who was kept incharge of the collected share and under whose guidance and supervision it was transported to the city. This tax was realized at the rate of one and a half *seer* per *kharwar* for the expenses of the said official. *Ibid.*
82. For meeeting the expenses of palace attendants and the subordinate staff of the revenue officials this cess was demanded at the rate of three *seers* per *kharwar*. *Ibid.* Mirza, *op.cit.*, Vol. II, f. 3-5.
83. Four *seers* were deducted from every *kharwar* for *Kardar, Ibid.*

Rusud-i-Deodi,[84] *Terazudari,*[85] *Quanongoi,*[86] *Dolljinsi,*[87] *Bhat Fund,*[88] *Zaffran,*[89] *Zari-Chopan,*[90] *Sakh-Shomari,*[91] *Zari-i-Murakab,*[92] *Zar-i- nikh,*[93] and *Rasum-i-Sabsi.*[94]Apart from all these ceses and taxes there was a large room for graft.

When Maharaja Ranbir Singh (1857-1885) took over the

---

84. *Rusudi-Deeodi* was a tax demanded form the revenue officials for the maintenance of palace at the rate of 2 to 3 hundred rupees. But these officialls like *Kardars, Thanedars,* expectedly charged this cess from the peasants. See also Mirza, *op.cit.*, Vol. II, ff. 3, 5, 6, 7, 9, 11.
85. One and a half *seer* was levied per *kharwar* for weignmon. Mizra, *Ibid.* Vol. II, f. 5.
86. One *trak per kharwar* was deducted for the *Qanongo Ibid.* See Mirza, *op.cit.*, Vol.I. See also Ramju Dhar, *op.cit.*, f.3.
87. From 1846 another cess was levied on Kashmir peasantry for maintenance of sepoy regiments, Mirza, *op.cit.*, Vol. II, ff. 6, 7-9.
88. For improving the condition of *Bhat* community of Jammu, a cess known as *Bhat Fund* was demanded from every Kashmr, *Ibid.*
89. It was a tax on saffron for which the valley was famouse. It was levied in addition to the usual state, share. *Foreign and Political A. July, 1863,* No. 73-75, N.A.I.
90. Even the cattle wealth of the peasant was not spared. 2½ annas were collected for heads for sheep and goats, Wazir Ratnu, Governor or Kashmir during Gulab Singh's time, collected 80,000 heads of shee and 16 *kharwars* of wool, although the total revenue fixed under this head was Rs 70,000 only. Mirza, *op. cit.*, Vol. I, ff. 18-19. In 1863 the amount collected under this head was Rs 80,000. *Foreign and Political A. July 1863,* No. 73-75., N.A.I.
91. It was a tax on buffaloes. *Ibid.*
92 It was a tax on ponies. *Ibid.* Mirza Saif-ud-Din, mentions it as *Zar-i-Nakhas* He says that even horse keepers had to supply horses or ponies as a tax. Here he refers to Shunga Kotwal who was extremely oppressive when he entered the stables he could take away any quota of horses he laid his hands on. Mirza, *op.cit.*, Vol. I, f. 3.
93 It was a tax on marriage. *Ibid.*
94. Though the vegetable growers were not charged for their produce but during Gulab Singh's time there is evidence to prove that even the vegetable growers and kitchen gardeners were not exempted from the net work of taxation. Sultan Pahalwan, to whom the revenues of the vegetable lands were formed out, paid the revenue of Rs 1200 annually, *Ibid.*, Vol. II, f. 7.

administration he laid down that peasants traders and all men of different professsions who were suffering from financial stress shall be granted remission in arrears outstanding against them, if they resumed their professions. But the magnitude of land revenue demand remained more or less the same.[95]

The state took there quarters of cash crops and pulses.[96] With regard to the system of *Trakee* a slight relaxation was made. Instead of four only two *traks* were charged and this system lasted upto 1960.[97] After 1860 attempts were made to introduce cash assessment but in vain. The assessment became heavier and resulted in further depressing the position of the peasant.[98] In 1869 there was a slight reduction and again only two extra *traks* were levied instead of four.[99] But the whole system was so full of absuses that no significant improvement was registered in the state's finances or in the condition of the peasantry.

In 1875 the harvest was a poor one but the state still took two shares of produce and left only one share to the peasant.[100] Next year in 1876 two *traks* per *kharwar* were again added to the assessment besides an aggregate cess

---

95. Mirza, *op.cit*, Vol. X, f. 316.
96. Lawrence, *Valley*, pp. 303-304
97. Pandits and Pirs were charged only one *trak*. A. Wingate, *op.cit.*, pp. 54-57.
 Majmu-i-Report of Jammu-va-Kashmir and Tibet (1873-75), p.33-35, *Gazetteer of Kashmir and Ladakh*, pp. 105-106.
98. Dewan Kripa Ram, *Majmu-i-Report* (1872-73), pp. 18-20. A. Wingate, *op.cit.*, pp. 55. S.N. Koul, *op.cit.*, p. 59. In 1870 *trakee* was reduced two *traks* but in 1872-73 it was again levied at the rate of five *traks* in some villages and in some at the rate of three *traks*.
99. *Majmu-i-Report of Jammu-va-Kashmir and Tibet*, pp. 30-33.
100. *Majmu-i-Report Jammu-va-Kashmir and Tibet*, (1873-75), pp. 32-34. A.Wingate, *op.cit.*, p. 55. Lawrence, *Valley*, p. 403. *Gazetteer of Kashmir and Ladakh*, p. 108.

which amounted to a *kharwar* and twelve *traks* per hundred *kharwars.*[101]

In 1877 bad weather added to excessive taxation. The assessment was delayed and the peasants preferred leaving their crops to rot in their fields. As a result, trade also came to stand still. Villages were deserted and people died of starvation.[102] This situation appears to have continued upto 1880. In 1880 under the *assamiwar khewat* the state share was made payable both in kind and cash.[103]

The state demand during Maharaja Partap Singh's reign was made payable partly in cash and partly in kind as a result of the cash crop settlement introduced by W.R. Lawrence. The state reduced the land revenue demand to 30 per cent of the gross produce.[104] However, in addition to it the *patwari* and *lambardari* cesses of two per cent and five per cent respectively were levied on each individual assessment.[105] In 1890-91 the custom of exempting villages from land revenue, belonging to influential persons, was abolished,[106] The attempts were made to assess the newly broken up waste lands.[107] However, the heavy receipts from these lands continued to fill the pockets of *patwaris* and Tehsil officials.[108]

---

101. A. Wingate, *op.cit.*, p. 55.
102. A. Wingate, *op.cit.*, pp. 54-56. Lawrence, *Valley*, pp. 446-47.
103. Ramju Dhar, *op.cit.*, ff. 8-10, S.N. Koul, *op.cit.*, pp. 58-59.
104. D.K. Palit, *op.cit.*, p. 91.
105. Lawrence, *Report on Position of cultivating classes in Kashmir, op.cit.* Younghusband, *op.cit.*, p. 197.
R.G. Wreford, *Census*, 1941, Vol. XXII., p. 15.
S.N. Koul, *op.cit.*, p. 59.
106. Pandit Bhag Ram, *Annual Administration Report of Jammu and Kashmir*, (1890-91), Jammu, 1892, p. 42.
107. *Ibid.*
108. *Ibid.*

TABLE 4

The following table shows the land revenue demand and collection of some years[109]

Year	*Demand*	*Amount collected*
1888-89	29,56,222	Not known
1889-90	31,72,977	Not known
1890-91	31,78,731	Not known
1891-92	31,87,812	Not known
1892-93	35,78,000	15,08,946
1893-94	32,96,187	14,54,352
1894-95	35,72,413	15,32,262
1895-96	15,36,324	14,92,070

In 1891-92 it was laid down that collection should be made in cash on an extensive scale in the newly assessed Tehsils. The unassessed Tehsils continued to make payments in kind as before according to an estimate made by *kardars* and provincial governors.[110] Attempts were made to check the mismanagement of grains received in land revenue. Steps were taken to recognize the grain department by placing it under the charge of the head treasurer *Wazir Bagju.*[111] The rules were laid down regulating the receipt of the quality of food grains paid by *Tehvildars* and putting a stop to thefts and illegal exactions.[112] But all these measures failed to meet the desired success due to the apathy of the governor and the dishonesty of his subordinate staff.[113]

---

109. These figures have been collected from the administrative reports of the given years available in Srinagar, Jammu and National Archives of India.
110. Bhag Ram Pandit, *Annual Administration Report of Jammu and Kashmir* (1891-92), pp. 34-39.
111. *Ibid.*, pp. 34-40.
112. *Ibid.*
113. *Ibid.*

Hence in spite of all these measures it was not until the second half of 20th century that a genuine effort was made to avoid confusion, secure confidence and attach peasants permanently to their holdings when a fair distribution of the produce between the state and the peasant took place.[114]

Revenue Functionaries

The valley of Kashmir was divided into various *parganas* and *wazarats* from time to time for purposes of revenue administration. Maharaja Gulab Singh in the beginning did not introduce any new system but allowed the valley to remain divided into different *parganas*, 36 in number.[115] After some time when he roughly estimated the fiscal condition of the valley he divided it into three main divisions and entrusted the administration of these three divisions to Wazirs-Ratnu, Narayan Bhan, Kanhaya Singh—and Pandit Raja Kak Dhar.[116] However, they not only neglected to undertake steps to improve agricultural production and thereby ameliorate the condition of the peasantry but equally ignored the increasing corruption in State's revenue department.[117] Their effort to obtain the Maharaja's favour adversely effected even the existing revenue collection machinery. To quote Maharaja Gulab Singh, "Owing to the activities of wazir Ratnu, the administration of the valley became defective and the

114. It was in 1950 that the big landed estates abolition act was passed with some other measures to provide relief to the peasants. See *Big landed estates abolition act*, 1950.

115 Mirza, *op.cit.*, Vol. I, f. 27

116. The civil administration was handed over to Kanhaya Singh and the military administration to Wazir Ratnu, *Ibid.*, Vol. I, ff. 26,29.

117. *Kotwal* Kanhaya without looking into the conduct of some of the *kardars*, dismissed them and gave birth to serious difficulties. As a result he was supplanted by Shunga *Kotwal* in early 1847. *Ibid.* Vol. I, f. 29.

revenue was not collected satisfactorily with the result the entire administration was in a shambles."[118]

This division of valley into three main units continued upto 1852 when again the valley was divided into seven main divisions. This time the administration was entrusted to :

(1) Pandit Raja Kak Dhar
(2) Wazir Punoo
(3) Wazir Zorawroo
(4) Mian Amir Singh
(5) Munshi Trilok Chand
(6) Colonel Beji Singh
(7) Janki Dass.[119]

All these above mentioned officials made the chief *jagirdars* of valley responsible for payment of revenue. The *jagirdars* on their part appointed *kardars* for collection of revenue. However, the whole system of revenue became more complicated, and workable only in the interest of corrupt revenue officials.[120]

Though there are scattered references in the records that Gulab Singh appointed adequate revenue staff and established the department of *Dobjinsi* (Department of revenue collection in kind), nothing appears to have been done which can be termed as definite.[121]

During Maharaja Ranbir Singh's time the whole valley was divided into *Wazarats* of *Shar-i-Khas*, Kamraj, Anantnag, Shupian and Pattan.[122] In 1880 this number of *Wazarats* was

118. *Ibid.*, Vol. I, f. 26.
119. *Ibid.*, Vol. I, f. 5.
120. Mirza, *op.cit.*, Vol. I, f. 3, Vol. II, f.175. See also *Ibid.* VII, ff. 130-133.
121. The other departments established by Maharaja Gulab Singh were those of *Dafta-i-Diwani* (the audit accounts department) and the *Daftar-i-Nizamat* the land record office. S.N. Koul, *Kashmir Economics*, p. 228.
122. Charles Girdlestone, *Memorendum on Kashmir*, pp. 7-8. C.E. Bates, *Gazetteer*, pp. 95-97. M.D. Fauq, *Rahnumai-Kashmir*, pp. 72-73.

further reduced to four by merging the *Wazarat* of Shupian together with Anantnag *Wazarat*.[123] Each *Wazarat* contained a number of Tehsils and was kept under the control of *Wazir Wazarat*.[124] This division continued down to Maharaja Pratap Singh's time. The head of the revenue department was *Hakim-i-Ala* or the governor of the province. Under him the executive control of the revenue department rested with *Diwam-i-Jins* or the revenue Commissioner.[125] Besides, the over-all supervision of the revenue department, his duties included transportation of grain to the public store houses, its distribution at fixed rates, and the maintenance of its account, with the help of subordinate staff.[126]

Then there were *Wazirs* of the *Wazarats*. The principle business of the *Wazirs* was the realization of revenue. According to Charles Girdlestone, "Wazir is the deputy commissioner of British territory, his charge being small his authority more restricted and duties less multifarious."[127]

He dealt with the revenue cases, the superintendence of roads, dispensaries, police and postal communication.[128] For the purpose of administration these *Wazarats* were further divided into *Tehsils* which were kept under the supervision and control of *Tehsildars*.[129]

Tehsildar: He generally fixed the yearly assessment of crops. It was upto *Tehsildar* and the establishment attached to him to take the final decision regarding the total produce of

---

123. M.D. Fauq, *Rahnumai Kashmir*, pp.72-73.
124. Charles Girdlestone, *op.cit.*, pp. 8-9.
125. Maharaja Gulab Singh always appointed his relatives and friends to this post. During his regime Mian Hattu Singh, Mian Ranbir Singh and Moti Singh of Poonch were appointed one after the other to this post. Mirza, *op.cit.*, Vol. VII, ff. 120,123 and 126.
126. *Ibid.*
127. Charles Girdlestone, *op.cit.*, pp. 8-10.
128. *Ibid.*, p. 8-10.
129. R.G. Wreford, *Census*, 1941, Vol. p. 14; P.N.K. Bamzai *op.cit.*, 687-89.

the village crop.[130] Evidently the avenues of graft open to him were enormous. He had under him a number of officials like, *Naib-i-Tehsildar, Thanedar, Kardar, Sazowul, Patwari, Muqadam, Shiqdar, Lambardar, Harkar* and *Tarazudar.*[131]

Naib Tehsildar or *(Naib-i-Zilla Sahib)* : He was put incharge of *Nayabat* (The group of villages) where the exercised his revenue and administrative functions. Maintaining the revenue records at *Nayabat* level. In this work he was assisted by *Sadr Daftri, Daftri* and *Khazanchi.*[132]

Thanedar: He was the chief official of the *pargana* who combined in himself both revenue and judicial authority. His duty was to look after the condition of the people in his jurisdiction and to report to the *Tehsildar* from time to time.[133] Besides he had the authority to decide the disputes that occured among the peasants. He had under him 40 to 50 sepoys called *Nizamat Paltan* who assisted the revenue officials at the time of assessment and collection. He possessed the power of giving minor punishments in case of fraud and deceit.[134]

Kardar: In the revenue machinery of the Dogras *Kardar* held a very important position. He had full authority for assessment and collection of the revenue. He used to superintend the crops before fixing the assessment. His establishment comprised *Parchanavis* (the record writer) *Tarazudar* etc.[135] It was in fact the duty of the *kardar* to maintain the record of peasants holdings and to submit them for inspection yearly, but he appears to have done this

---

130. Charles Girdlestone, *op.cit.*, pp. 8-10.
131. *Ibid.*, P.N.K. Banzai, *op.cit.*, pp. 687-89
132. Charles Girdlestone, *op.cit.*, pp. 8-10.
133. P.N.K. Bamzai, *op.cit.*, 687-89; R.K. Parmu, *History of Dogra Rule*, Ms. p. 72.
134. Lawrence, *Valley*.
135. R. Thorp, *Kashmir Misgovernment*, p. 2.

job very rarely during the period of our study. Though their pay was included in the *trakee*, they used to charge an extra share for themselves at the time of harvesting.[136] These *kardars* used to demand *salamana* from the peasants individually on festive occasions like *Desera* and *Nouroz* (the new years day).[137] In 1860 these were replaced by *chakladars*.[138]

Sazawul: He was usually incharge of ten villages and his duty was to supervise the work of *Shiqdar* (the watchmen of crops) and to report to the *kardar*.[139] To quote R. Thorp, "It is said that he (Sazawul) commonly extorted money from the villages."[140]

Patwari: His duty was to keep a separate register wherein the entries of all *jagirdars* and the tenants under them were being entered. In every village there was a Patwari or the village accountant.[141] There is reference in records to *Mir Patwari* also who was the head of seven *Patwaris* and used to inspect their work.[142]

Tehildar: He was the official incharge of the storage of the paddy which was collected from the peasants as the state share. Secondly it was his duty to make arrangement for the transportation of the procured paddy to the city.[143]

Muqadam: He was the village headman. His duty was to

---

136. *Ibid.*, F. Hentry, *op.cit.*, 1882; C. E. Bates, *Gazetteer*, pp. 95-97; Bamzai *op.cit.*, p. 689.
137. H.M. Lawrence, *op.cit.*, Section C, 28 Jan. 1848, file Nos. 33-44, J.
138. Mirza, *op.cit.*, I.f.106. H.L.P. Wynne, *Report on Kashmir*, For Pol. A. file Nos. 343-49, Jan. 1873, N.A.I.
139. Bates, *Gazetteer*, pp. 95-97; Charles Girdlestone, *op.cit.*, pp. 8-10.
140. Charles Girdlestone, *op.cit.*, pp. 8-10. R. Thorp, *op.cit.*, p.4.
141. *Ibid.*, p. 3. *Gazetteer of Kashmir and Ladakh*, p. 110, Bamzai, *op.cit.*, Vol. I, f. 27.
142. Mirza, *op.cit.*, Vol. I, f.27.
143. H.M. Lawrence, *op.cit.*, Section C, 28 Jan. 1848, file Nos. 33-44, Jammu Archives.

keep an eye on theft in the village. He also used to provide assistance to revenue officials during the period of collection.[144]

Shiqdar: A village could have anywhere between one and four *shiqdars*, depending upon its size. His duty was to watch the crops until the state collected her share. It is said that *shiqdars* extorted money from peasants by threatening to accuse them of stealing grain.[145]

Lambardar: He was the hereditary tax collector of villages and was responsible to *Tehsildar* for the revenues of villages which he collected. Besides the usual pay he retained 2 per cent of the revenue from the collected sum as reward for his labour. He was the also responsible for making necessary arrangements for such officials and visitors as entered the village.[146] E.F. Knight says, "It is he who too often receives the pay of these (coolies working under him), and how much he retains as his *Dastur* and how much he hands over to them is difficult to say. In some villages he is not much below the village scape-goat and a powerful lambardar would never render the state its due."[147]

Harkar: He was a police constable. In every twenty villages there used to be a *Harkar's* house. All the male members in his family were *Harkars*. His duty was to report secretly the transactions in the village. He also gave directions to the other revenue officials and to the *Doom*

---

144. *Gazetteer of Kashmir and Ladakh.*, p. 110. C.E.bates, *Gazetteer, op.cit.*, p. 97.; R. Thorp, *op.cit.*, p. 3.
145. According to Lawrence he received eight *kharwars* of *Shali* (paddy) from village and took twelve *kharwars from the State.* Lawrence, *Valley*, p. 402.
146. Maharaja Pratap Singh, *Diary of an inspection tour to Gilgit*, p. 22., Jammu Archives.
147. E.F. Knight, *Where three Empires Meet*, London, 1905, pp. 64-65.

community (the watchmen of villages).[148] *Tarazudar:* He was simply a weighman and was always n attendance upon *Kardar* and *Tehvildar* when the state commenced collection of revenue. He was the chief, though lowly, instrument of exploiting the peasant on behalf of the State, for it was he who overweighed the produce to extract a large revenue. There is evidence that sometimes instead of a *kharwar* of sixteen *traks* he took from the peasants a *kharwar* of 18 *traks.*[149]

All these officials appear to have been paid by the state meagrely in kind and then irregularly. This may have justified in their eyes their taking resort to corruption, though they were not the only ones steeped in corruption.

Working of the Land Revenue Administration

The land revenue demand and the taxes and cesses actually realized were far in excess of those that finally went into the treasury. The whole work of realization was in the hands of a machinery that was corrupt from top to bottom. It was very rarely that the incidence of *trakee* was actually reduced to two *traks* per *kharwar*. As though this was not enough, there were revenue payments and other *Abwabs* to be paid to the state officials. Lawrence wrongly remarks that only air and water are exempted from taxation.[150]

As a result of these heavy demand of the revenue officials the peasants were often forced to give up the cultivation and consequently payments fell into arrears. In

---

148. H.M. Lawrence *op.cit.*, Section C., 28 January, 1848, file Nos. 33-44, Jammu Archives. This *doom* community was generally fed by peasants of villages. It may be noted that after many land reforms the *doom* community is still landless and works as agricultural labourers and watchmen in villages.

149. *Ibid.*, R. Thorp, *op.cit.*, p.4.

150. Lawrence, *Valley*, p. 417.

1851, 30 lakhs of rupees were in arrears because most of the peasants left their lands due to extortionate demands of the state and its officials.[151]

In 1852 the revenue which was in arrears was assigned to the army as their salary but the condition of the country was so bad that they could not collect more than 8,000 rupees.[152] The financial statements of Munshi Trilok Chand indicate that in1852 the arrears amounted to 15,00,000 with a revenue deficit of 23,00,000.[153]

In 1857 when Ranbir Singh became Maharaja of Kashmir, and order was issued that all arrears if not paid by *Nouroz* (the new years day) may be charged interest at the rate of two rupees in cash and two *kharwars* of rice for every hundred per month.[154]

In some villages the *chakladar* applied and got land which he afterwards abandoned. The village in which the land was situated was held responsible for payment of the revenue assessed on *chak*.[155] The peasants of the village neither took possession nor paid the land revenue but the amount was entered against them as arrears.[156] Often the *mustajirs* made a bid for a village and offered a large increase on fixed

---

151. There was a deficit of 5 lakhs of rupees, Maharaja Gulab Singh adviced Dewan Jowala Sahai and Mian Ranbir Singh, his son, to whom the revenue administration had been entrusted to make the remission of three to four thousand rupees so that this concession could ensure the collection of some amount of revenue. Mirza, *op.cit.*, Vol. IV, f. 114. See also *Ibid.*, Vol. V.f.8.
152. *Ibid.*, Vol. V., f.8.
153. *Ibid.*, f. 62.
154 *Ibid.*, Vol. VI, f. 6.
155. W.R. Lawrence, *Assessment report of Ich-Nagam Tehsil 1891*, Jammu Archives, pp. 2-6.
156. *Ibid.* There are various such instances in records both Persian and English *Karvai-jalsa Council Aliya Jammu-va-Kashmir*, 1898-1908, State Archives,, Srinagar.

TABLE 5

The following table shows how the collections had fallen during Ranbir Singh's time in 252 villages for which information is available owing to the contraction of the arable.[157]

The figures appended below show the totals

Year	*Actual demand for 252 villages*	*Actual collection from 252 villages*
1880	3,88,613	3,45,031
1881	3,96,274	3,51,547
1882	4,23,440	6,53,673
1883	4,64,200	2,44,389
1884	4,69,701	4,09,562
1885	4,36,872	1,97,841
1886	4,41,357	2,31,550
1887	4,41,403	2,48,369
Total	34,61,904	23,81,962

revenue. They remained in a village for three or four years of good harvest, embezzled large sums of money out of the amount the villagers had paid as revenue and subsequently these were entered as arrears against the village.[158]

The *mustajir* collected half the crops and even more, as his share. In some villages arrears of revenue outstanding against the peasants were added to the fraudulent accounts of *Patwaris* and *Lambardars* whose records were seldom straight and reliable.[159]

---

157. A. Wingate, *op.cit.*, pp. 60-67.
In these circumstances both the peasant and the state had to suffer losses but between the two the peasant appears to have, suffered more than State. He was left with as little as was perhaps sufficient to keep his body and soul together.

158. *Ibid.*

159. A. Wingate states on the basis of his information that the *Patwari* carried three editions of his records and all on scraps of paper one of them was meant for himself, one for the *Tehsildar* and the third one for villagers. A. Wingate, *op.cit*, p. 49.

In *pargana Dansu* the peasants had paid the revenue in full for the period 1880-1888; still Rs 31,747 were shown as outstanding against them.[160] The *mustajir* had paid the state demand in full but at the same time succeeded in taking from the treasury an equivalent sum in the form of agricultural loan on behalf of peasants. However, in actual practice it was never advanced to the peasant but only entered against each on paper or sold in the market or to their relatives at a high rate.[161]

The system of management of the water-nuts (Singhara) called *Mahal-i-Singhara* was no less oppressive. The peasants could hardly afford bare subsistence. It was customary to lease out surface covered by waternuts called Mahal through public action. The highest bidder got the lease and entered into contract with the government. He employed the labourers from surrounding areas where the picking, extraction and collection of *singharas* had become a profession through generations. The labourers, after spending weeks together in water, handed over *singharas* to the contractor and in return got very little wages or sometimes nothing.[162]

No less oppressive was the system practised for the

---

160. W.R. Lawrence, *Assessment Report of Ich-Nagam Tehsil, 1891*, Jammu Archives, pp. 5-6.
161. H.M. Lawrence, *Transfer of Govt. to Maharaja Gulab Singh of Kashmir*, Secton D, 28 Jan., 1848, file Nos. 33-34, Jammu Archives.
Majmu-i-Report Jammu-va-Kashmir and Tibet, (1877-78), pp. 21-22.
Even if a peasant did not take loan for agricultural operations, the state officials demanded one *Trak* as an item of kharch for the agricultural loan. Generally 2 *seers* were demanded as a tax for agricultural loan by state from each *kharwar* of produce, H.M. Lawrence. *op.cit.*
162. *Ibid.*
Mirza, *op.cit.*, Vol. I., ff. 7-9. See also M.M.A. Beg, *Zara-i-Islahat*, pp. 45-47.

collection of Saffron. Saffron fields were not assessed like the other cash crops where the State share was collected straightaway in cash. Instead the share due to the State amounting to more than half the produce was auctioned to a contractor, who himself arranged to collect the share at the harvest time. The peasant who worked for the contractor got a handful of salt in return.[163]

Here it becomes clear that the revenue system in Kashmir continued to vitiate he entire system of agrarian economy in the region; possibly payment in fixed cash assessment might have mitigated the impact of corruption to some extent.[164]

Lastly came the taxes on handicrafts. These too were exacted with much severity and oppression. But the burden of these taxes most likely fell on those peasants who tried to supplement their income from land with income from wool manufactures, wood work and embroidery.[165] Very likely some of the revenues collected from this source must have stuck of official's fingers. There was of course hardly any person who could escape the

---

163. The state share was nominally half the crop but the villagers asserted that after satisfying the corrupt officials only a quarter of the crop remained with them. Ramju Dhar, *Kaifaiyat-Intizam Mulk-i-Kashmir*, f. 3. Dewan Anant Ram, *op.cit.*, pp. 105-06. *A note on Jammu and Kashmir State*, p. 29.
164. In fact Lachman Dass is an extreme example of what must have been a type among the high officials. Payment of land revenue in cash was the one form that could have benefitted the peasant; but then the officials such as Lachman Dass were dead set against such assessment. Dewan Lachman Dass, *Petition against cash assessment*, 1896, *op.cit.*, Jammu Archives.
165. Because mostly the peasants of small holdings engaged themselves in handicrafts during winter months. Charles Girdlestone, *op.cit.*, pp. 30-32.

net-work of the taxation system.[165] To quote Vigne, "Even the grave digger and the dancing girls were not exempted from the taxation."[167]

Hence until the commencement of the land settlement and fixed cash assessment of revenue in the year 1889, Kashmir was never subject to a regular fixed assessment. These peasants remained always uncertain of their future liabilities. From the time of Maharaja Gulab Singh the crude system of fluctuating assessments not regulated by any recognized theory of principle but mainly depending on the will of *kardars,* the provincial governors and their subordinate staff was in vogue to the great detriment of the cultivating class. Every years the provincial governors enhanced the demand irrespective of the paying capacities of the peasant, simply to show a thriving budget estimate.[168] As a result of this large balances accrued against the peasants and the state officials pocketed heavy illegal exactions.

The arbitrariness of the entire administrative machinery was exemplified by Gulab Singh's own conduct, who could be approached irrespective of time and place. All one was

---

166. Men of all professions were taxed. In 1847 the sum of Rs. 120 was fixed as a professional tax on shoe makers. Though they made a representation to Sahaz Ram Trisal the Assistant of Raja Kak Dhar but nothing was done to relieve them from this burden. Insteed each of them was handed over a chit showing the amount that he had to pay.
According to revenue schedule of 1848, Rs 8,500 were collected from butchers as a professional tax. The boatmen were charged six to eight rupees per adult and Rs. 4 to 6 per minor. All non-agriculturists had to pay *Baj* and *Kharaj*. Mirza, *op.cit.*, Vol. I, ff. 62-64. See also Vol. II f.7, 27 and Vol. VII, f. 64 of the same.
167. G.T. Vigne, *Travels,* Vol. I, p.119. This statement is supported by Mirza Saif-ud-Din also. See Mirza, *op.cit.*, Vol. II, ff. 40-44.
168. Pandit Bhag Ram, *Annual Administration Report of Jammu and Kashmir 1889-90.*

required to do was to hold a rupee in his hand and cry, "Maharaja, arz hai", tender the rupee and obtain the Maharaja's decision spontaneously.[169] No method was allowed to establish itself whereby default or fraud in the revenue machinery could be prevented.[170]

169. Mirza, *op.cit.*, Vol. VII, ff. 55,57,175,176. See K.M. Panikar, *Maharaja Gulab Singh; the founder of Jammu and Kashmir State*, p. 149.

170. Charles Girdlestone, *op.cit.*, pp. 3-8. *Imperial Gazetteer of India*, Vol.XV, pp. 136-137. Wreford, *Census*, 1941, Vol. p. 14. See also O.N.Dhar, 'Land Reforms in Kashmir" *Indian Affairs Record*, Vol. III., No. 4, Delhi, 1954, p. 475. Lawrence, *Valley*, pp. 418-21.

4
Land Revenue Assignees and Other Grantees

The System of assigning large and small tracts of land and its revenue to members of various social classes appears to have been in vogue in ancient Kashmir.[1]

During the Sultanate period (1320-1586) there are frequent references to show that land was assigned to *ummra and ulema* who assisted the king in carrying out the administration.[2] *Nayakas* are referred to as the military chiefs who held lands for maintaining retainers to

---

1. Such large assignments were made in Kashmir during the reign of *Suganda* (904-906 A.D.) *Chakravarman* (936-937 A.D.) and Ananta (1028-1062 A.D.).
   Kalhana, *Rajatarangini* (Emg. Tr.) M.A. Stein, Vol.I, London, 1900 (Book seventh), pp. 218-287. See also nn. 161, 162, 249, 301. This fact of giving land assignments for various services is also mentioned in connection with the office of *Akspatala*. According to one view the *Akspatala* is mentioned as a court of justice but the more authentic version would make us believe that *Akspatala was* the office of accountant general where the land grants *Pathopadhyaya* were executed by recorder of official documents, *Ibid;* Vol. I, p. 223, n. 301. See also S.C. Ray, *History and Culture of Kashmir*, Delhi, pp. 143-144.
2. R.K. Parmu, *History of Muslim Rule in Kashmir,*, pp. 399-400.

safeguard against foreign invasions.[3]

In the wake of its conquest by Emperor Akbar in 1586 A.D., Kaṣhmir was made a Sarkar of the province of Kabul. The lands of Kashmir were assessed for higher rates than had hither to been charged and the whole land was declared to be the Crown land.[4]

The Afghan rulers of Kashmir (1753-1818) followed the Mughal system and no material change seems to have been effected except for the fact that they replaced the Mughal governors and officials of administration with counterparts appointed by them.[5]

From 1819 to 1846 Kashmir remained part of the Sikh empire. Ranjit Singh is said to have resumed all asṣignments of land granted by his predecessors and reduced the landed aristocracy to a low ebb.[6] To quote Moorcraft "When country came into hands of Sikhs, Ranjit Singh made a general resumption and ousted the possessors of grantees of land of every class, thus

---

3. Jonaraja, *Rajatarangini*, Vol.III, Eng. tr. J.C. Dutt., Calcutta, 1889, p. 66. See also *Tuhfat-ul-Abwab* (Per.Ms.) Anonymous, Research Department Library, Srinagar, p.64.
4. Soon after the conquest of Kashmir Akbar found that the inquiry into the sources and the amount of revenues of Kashmir caused deep discontent to Mirza Yusuf Khan, the first governor of Kashmir. He made it clear to the Emperor that there was every possibility of revolt. Yusuf Khan considered himself incapable of resolving this question and resigned.
   Abul Fazal, *Akbar-nama*, English tr. by Hentry Beveridge, 3 vols. Calcutta, 1897, Vol. III, pp. 827-30. Sir W. Haig, *The Cambridge History of India*, ed. by Sir R. Burn, Delhi 1957, Vol.IV, pp. 136-140.
5. Moorcraft G. Trebeck, *Travels.*, Vol. II, p. 125. It is stated that every governor used to appoint his own Secretarial staff which is explained from the Kashmiri proverb "Yelih Yamsund Subahdar Telih Tamsund peshkar" i.e. Every Subahdar had his own Secretarial staff. See R.K. Parmu, History of Muslim Rule in Kashmir, p. 402.
6. See *Khalsa Durbar Records*, Punjab State Archives, Patiala Bundle No. 5, Vol. XIII, pp. 323-327.

summarily reducing thousands, who had long lived in comfort, to a state of absolute destitution."[7]

During the period of our study the revenue assignees and grantees of Kashmir were *jagirdars, muafidars* and *chakdars.*[8]

Jagirdars: The contemporary estimates do not figure out the exact number of *jagirdars* nor the actual amount of land that they held. After taking charge of Kashmir, Gulab Singh made investigations into *jagirs* which had been

---

7. Moorcraft, *op.cit.*, Vol. I, p. 125. Here this resumption should not be taken to mean that Ranjit Singh wanted to invent a new device of payment for rendering of military or non-military service; he merely wanted to plant his own landed aristocracy there. He was assisted by his own Dewans who he gave *jagirs* in return for civil or military assistance. One jagir assignment worth Rs. 6000 rupees was assigned to Dewan Dinanath in the Kashmir Province. See Shamat ali. *Sikhs and Afghans*, p. 36, Patiala, 1848. See also Indu Banga, *Agrarian System of Sikhs*, Delhi, 1978, p. 124.
8. The difference in the class of these assignees was due to the nature of the assignment that each one of them *(jagirdar, muafidar, chakdar)* held. It is very relevant to point it out here that the institution of the *jagir* was not unknown in ancient Kashmir. During ancient period we find *Nayaks* appropriating and collecting land revenue and in return keeping the country in order and maintaining a body of troops, for civil and military service. Kalhana, *op.cit.*, Vol. I, p. 354.
   Under the Mughals when the reorganization of administration took place, this system of land assignments to nobles and courtiers became a regular part of Mughal administration and thereby came to be organized into a well developed system.
   See also Baden, Powell, *The Land Systems of British India*, Delhi, 1967, Vol. I, pp. 528-29. The *Muafidars* were such grantees as received rent free lands from the state. Such grants were made even in ancient times mainly to religious personages and charitable institutions. Kalhana, *op.cit.*, Vol. I, pp. 15-20. D.D. Kosambi, *Origins of Feudalism in Kashmir. Journal of Bombay Royal Asiatic Society*, 15th Anniversary Bombay 1965, p. 120.
   The *chakdari system is of very recent origin. The state in a bid* to restore waste lands assigned sizeable tracts to the state officials for their services.

granted by his predecessors.[9] In order to have effective control over the civil and military administration of Kashmir Maharaja Gulab Singh resumed some of the *Jagirs.*[10] However, serious opposition came from various quarters like Hazara and Muzaffarabad and from other hill chiefs. Finally Maharaja Gulab Singh came to the conclusions after negotiating with the British authorities at Lahore, that the resumed jagirs and *muafis* should all be released to restore peace in Kashmir.[11] Hence a policy of reconciliation was followed and *jagirs* were released and granted to *jagirdars* for rendering military and civil services. The military service was rendered by the three Bomba Rajas belonging to Kathai, Dupatta and Muzaffarabad. They were asked to pay a revenue of Rs. 9000

---

9. Major-General D.K. Palit, *Jammu and Kashmir Arms*, Dehradun, 1972, p. 49.
10. Foreign Deptt. Sec. Dec. 1846, file No. 1266, N.A. I.
11. When the adminstration of Kashmir was handed over to Maharaja Gulab Singh the turbulent hill tribes of Hazara aand Muzaffarabad rose in revolt against his authority. The ill equipped 7000 troops of the Maharaja were defeated by the armed troops of Hazara and Muzaffarabad. Maharaja Gulab Singh anxiously requested the British government at Lahore for exchange of territories of Hazara and Balkot with some portions of territory lying in the plains on river Jehlum. The British attitude was in the beginning uncompromising and they asked the Maharaja to release all *jagirs* and *muafis* which he had resumed. After issuing the orders of release a treaty was signed by Maharaja Gulab Singh and Lahore Darbar on 25th may 1847. Under this treaty the Maharaja received the districts of Munawar, Sujanpore and Pathankot in exchange for the districts of Hazara and Balkot. After some time the Maharaja had to surrender Sujanpore and Pathankot and retained only a part of Munawar and the districts of Kathua and Suchetgarh. According to Henery Lawrence this arrangement was made with the intention of paying Rs 56,000 annually to the hill chiefs of Rajouri, Basoli, Jasrota, Ramnagar and Kishtwar, who preferred to live under British protection and not as the subjects of the Maharaja; *Lahore Political Diaries*, III. p. 66. 143-148.

annually and had to maintain 5000 armed retainers.[12] The Khakha chief of Buniar, Chikar, Kotli, Dhana and Uri had to maintain 7000 armed troops and to pay Rs. 14,000 as annual revenue.[13]

The leading *jagirdars* rendering civil service to Maharaja Gulab Singh were:[14]

(1) Pandit Kamal Bhan
(Chief Record Keeper)
(2) Munshi Trilok Chand
(Chief Treasurer)
(3) Hakim Azim
(Chief Physician)
(4) Lachman Pandit Dhar
(Governor of Kashmir)
(5) Wazir Ratnu
(Kotwal)
(6) Ganesha
(Chief Toshkhana).

Besides these the *jagirdars* of Maharaja included Wazir Punoo, Wazir Zorawroo and Raja Kak Dhar.[15]

---

12. *Arzi* submitted by Hill chiefs to Henery Lawrence, For. Sec. Cons. File No. 1125, Dec. 26, 1846, N.A.I.
13. For supplementing the military requirements of the Maharaja in Kashmir, there were seven regiments of artillery. The total number of regiments was 600 of all ranks, three regiments of infantry with 1000 *sawars*. Besides this regular and irregular army, army of 2500 persons armed with fire-locks and swords was provided by tributary chiefs, *Jagirdars* and hill chiefs of Kaghan, Uttarmachipora and Karna.
H.M. Lawrence's *Report from Kashmir*, dated Nov. 15, 1847, For. Sec. Cons. file No. 1243-47, N.A.I.
See also *Taylor's Report*, dated September 27, 1847. For Pol. Cons. No. 452-53, dated Dec 30. 1848, N.A.I.
14. Mirza Saif-ud-Din, *Akhbarat*, Vol.I, ff. 2-6.
See also Vol. V. of *Akhbarat*, ff. 21-23.
15 *Ibid*.

Every *jagirdar* had certain villages wholly or partially assigned to him as *jagir*.[16] He used to get the revenue of these *jagir* villages directly. Usually the *jagirdar* took away 75 per cent of the produce and left the remaining 25 per cent to the *zamindar*.[17] The *jagir* assignments included not only land taxes but also customs and market duties, forest revenues and judicial fines.[18] These *jagirdars* exacted the payment not in the form of agricultural commodities alone but also of forest, cottage industry products animals and so

---

16. Besides the people who were in active service of the Maharaja there were a few who were considered to be loyal to the Maharaja and enjoyed *jagir* holdings, as a sign of loyality. These people used to maintain retainers. These loyal persons were given *mukararee* or cash grants also for the maintenance of the retainers. These loyal *jagirdars* of Dogra rulers were known as Double *Tazimi Sardars*. Though these double *Tazimi sardars* were not bound to maintain retainers for the king but being the confidents of the king maintained these retainers out of courtesy. No decision could be taken without seeking their opinion on administrative matters. None of the *patta* or records states the number of retainers which were maintained by *jagirdars* and *double tazimi sardars. List of Ruling Princes, Chiefs and Leading personages in Jammu and Kashmir State and Gilgit agency* (Govt. Publication), Delhi, 1939, pp. 10-12 (available in N.A.I.)
17. Significantly the term *zamindar* in Kashmir has invariably been used to denote the tiller of the soil whether he had his own land or was absolutely landless. In view of the fact that the *zamindar* has a special connotation in medieval Indian parlance where he held superior rights in land. There is always a possibility of this term being misconstrued in the context of Kashmir. We came across a number of references both in Persian and English records where it has been used to refer to the tiller of soil and him alone.
18. *Farman, regarding jagir with cash and kind in Martand and Devasar in favour of Raja Kak Dhar 1905*, v.s. The Farman is in possession of Pt. S.L. Dhar, Dalgate Bolouvard Road, Srinagar. Shri Dhar has a huge collection of more than 25 documents which are mostly in the form of *bia-namas*, letters, *Farmans* and orders dealing mostly with the grant and release of *jagirs*. I am extremely grateful to him for letting me consult this *farman* and some other documents.

on.[19] The absence of a well developed administrative and judicial system gave an ample opportunity to *jagirdars* for tapping non-agricultural sources of revenue.[20] Legislative and judicial remedies were provided only in the last quarter of the 19th century. Inside jagir lands a *jagirdar* could exact grazing fee on the cattle in the same manner in which he recovered the land revenue. Within his jagir, the right of the land holder dying heirless, instead of escheating to the State devolved on the *jagirdar*.[21] Apart from this the State lands given on rent entitled him to receive the rent. Besides the income from water mills within his *jagir* accrued to him.[22] He also had the power to exercise his choice in appointing the village headman.[23] Generally speaking the *jagirdar* enjoyed higher prospects than were indicated in *patta* granted to him. Even in the event of crop failure *jagirdars* appear never to have allowed appropriate remissions to the peasants. Ordinarily a *jagirdar* could appropriate an income which was several times higher than the salary pertaining to his position. They preferred land assignments to cash salaries because the land assignments were subject to

---

19. *Chief Secretariate Pol. and Genl. Deptt. file No. 76 of 1876*, J.K.. Here it is of interest to note that if a small river passed through the *jagir* lands, the presants cultivating these lands had to provide fish to the *jagirdar* irrespective of whether the river bred the fish or not. See *Karvai-Jalsa-Council-Aliya Riyasat Jammu-va-Kashmir*, Jan. 1898, J.K.
20. Mirza Saif-ud-Din, *Akhbarat*, Vol. I,. f. 166.
21. Some of the *jagirs* were assigned on a hereditary basis. *See Pata regarding grant of jagir of Kava Chak illaqa on hereditary basis in the name of Pandit Raja Kak Dhar, 1863*. The photocopy of the *patta* was consulted from Mr. Sham Sundar Lal Dhar's collections. In fact there are various such instances in records.
    See also *list of Ruling princes chiefs and leading personages in Jammu & Kashmir State and Gilgit Agency*, pp. 7-15.
22. *Patta regarding grant of jagir in Nunar Illaqa in favour of Pandit Raja Kak Dhar*, Jan. 1857.
23. *Chief Sec. Pol. and Genl. Dept. file No. 76*, 1896.

various arbitrary exactions unlike the fixed cash salaries. No doubt the agricultural rents were paid only once but there were other customary payments made to *jagirdar* on different festivals etc.[24] The chief *jagirdars* responsible for revenue appointed their own *kardars* in their *jagirs* to collect the revenue and to administer the *pargana*. The *Dastural Amal* of Main Singh states that in the year 1847 A.D. all *jagirs* were in the grip of *kardars*, the assessors of revenue and sepoys were despatched to villages for the security of revenue.[25] These *jagirdars* were allowed considerable latitude in their treatment of the peasantry.

The peasants of *jagir* lands appear to have often lost all attraction for cultivation during the Dogra period. At times they were forced by the sepoys to carry on cultivation because their negligence must have resulted in the fall of State revenue.[26]

During Maharaja Pratap Singh's rule a committee was appointed to look into *jagirs* and *muafilands*. The committee instead of giving relief to the peasants from the burden of landed aristocracy, strengthened the exploitative structure by introducing a new class of landholders who

---

24. Mirza Saif-ud-Din, *op.cit.*, Vol.. I, f. 27.
25. This was an ancient practice. We have evidence to prove that the military force of *Ekangas* was attached to the *Akspatala* (office where *pattas* or documents regarding the grant of land *pattapodhyaya* were executed). See Kalhana, *op.cit.*, Vol. III, pp. 223-24, n. 301. Likewise during Dogra period the *Daftar-i-Nizamat* (office dealing with land revenue and its administration) had under its control military force called *Nizamat Paltan* which closely corresponds to that of *Ekangas*. *Ibid*. Lawrence, *Valley*, p. 305.
26. In 1852, 300 sepoys were despatched to the *jagir* of Pandit Raja Kak Dhar, 400 to the *jagir* of Wazir Punoo, 30 to that of Wazir Zorawroo, 12 to the *jagir* of Munshi Trilok Chand and 40 to the *jagir* of Mian Amir Singh to make the peasants work on their lands from morning till evening. Mirza, *op.cit.*, Vol. IV, ff. 114-115.

also held *pattas* and therefore came to be known as *pattadars.*[27] These *pattadars* were persons who enjoyed *jagirs* below Rs. 3000.[28]

This type of *pattadar,* who was only an assignee of revenue and had no proprietory rights, used to recover the rent in kind as a result of some special privileges granted to him.[29] Besides these privileges the *pattadars* were give the right to recover all arrears of *jagir* money from the peasants as arrears of land revenue. The *pattadars* mostly rendered civil services.

However, under this *jagir* system the peasant was not only exposed to the land revenue demand but was subjected to innumerable legal and illegal exactions. Besides, the ususal land revenue demand these *jagirdars* levied a number of cesses like *Nehri*[30], *maswarichamvar,*[31] *maswaridom*[32], *Nazar-sayeer,*[33] *Banor,*[34] *kama,*[35] *Hari-*

---

27. M.M.A .Beg, *Zarai-Islahat,* pp. 8-9.
28. *Karvai-Jalsa Council Aliya Riyasat Jammu-va-Kashmir,* Jan., 1898-1900, pp. 62-65.
29. *Ibid.*
30. This cess was realized at the rate of one *pai* for every kharwar *i.e.* two *maunds* and was realized to defray expenses of feeding jagirdar during his stay in the village for the purpose of collection. *Levy of cesses in and reassessment of jagirs in the State and validity of pattas granted,* Chief Sec. Pol. and Genl. Dept. file No. 76 of 1896, Jammu Archives, pp. 20-21.
31. This was levied at the rate of 3 *pais* for each holding for the payment of men who supplied firewood and fodder to *jagirdar* and performed other services for him, *Ibid.*
32. This was levied for *Doom* for keeping strict watch of the harvest of *jagirdars, Ibid.*
33. This cess was levied during the kharif harvest from four annas to four rupees for the horses maintained by *jagirdar,* if any, *Ibid.*
34. It was realized at the rate of four annas to one rupee during the *Rabi* season. (purpose is not known), *Ibid.*
35. The rate of the realization of this cess varied from place to place. It was realized from four annas to 28 rupees, *Ibid.* (purpose not known)

nazrana,[36] *Thakur,*[37] *khalna,*[38] *malba,*[39] *nanwan,*[40] *muqadami,*[41] *jhuwar,*[42] *sunhar,*[43] *begaree,*[44] *Batwal,*[45] *Jogi,*[46] *Chowkidar,*[47] *Zohar*[48] and *Tarkhan.*[49] These cesses were recovered by the *jagirdar* before the distribution of crop.

Hence though the *jagirdari* system rendered military and non-military assistance in several capacities to the State under the Dograss, it generally tended towards

---

36. This cess was levied from four annas to six rupees during *Kharif* season, *Ibid,* (purpose not known)
37. This was levied at the rate of one *topa* for each *Gumao* as an indication of *Haq-i-milkiat* (which practically they never possessed). *Ibid.*
38. The purpose of this cess is not clear from the documents but it was realized at the rate of two *topas* for each *Gumao, Ibid.*
39. This cess was realized with the intention of defraying miscellaneous expenses of the village at the rate of one *topa* for each *Gumao.* However, this cess did not benefit the *jagirdar* in any way, *Ibid.*
40. This cess was levied at the rate of two *topas* for each Gumao, *Ibid.* (purpose not known).
41. This cess was realized for *Muqadams* to whom *jagirdar* paid only one topa though he realized 3 topas for each *Gumao, Ibid.*
42. The tax was levied on account of wages for the carriers engaged by *jagirdar* for carrying the produce to his own place at the rate of one-fourth of a topa, *Ibid.*
43. For meeting the expenses of the gold-smith, the *jagirdar* levied a separate cess at the rate of one-fourth of a topa, *Ibid.*
44. The *jagirdar* paid nothing to *Begarees* (the forced labourers) though he ostensibly realized two topas for each *Gumao, Ibid.*
45. One topa on each *Gumao* was realized for the maintenance of the *Batwal* who was the personal chowkidar of the *jagirdar, Ibid.*
46. *Jagirdar* realized half a topa from each *Gumao* for persons who were supposed to have power of preventing hailstorms. *Ibid.*
47. This cess was levied for the payment to *Chowkidars,* whom *jagirdars,* however, paid nothing. It was realized half a topa for each *Gumao, Ibid.*
48. This cess was levied on account of payment made by *jagirdar* to iron smiths and carpenters in the service of the *jagirdar* irrespective of whether he paid them anything or not, *Ibid.*
49. In addition to all these cesses, four annas were annually deducted from the peasants as *nazar sayer,* etc. *Ibid.*

accentuating social injustices in course of time. Few and far between were the occassions when *jagirs* were bestowed for military services. The fact is that impact of British necessitated the reorganization of armed forces of the State.[50] The system of maintenance of retainers was progressively abandoned in favour of regular and well trained armies by the State. Army personnel were now paid salaries from the State exchequer.

Some of the *jagirs*, were still in existence until recently.[51] Since the *jagirdari* system was loosing its importance and the number of *jagirs* was on the wane, little care was taken to maintain regular records of *jagirs* and *jagirdars* and their doings in the *jagirs*.

During the reign of Maharaja Pratap Singh (1885-1925) the State army came to be reorganized on modern lines. The British Government of India lent their senior army officers to train and discipline the State armed forces; not infrequently were the British top brass appointed to head the State forces.[52] Obviously the practice of basing the better disciplined and modernized army on an out dated exploitative institution of jagirdari must have looked absurd. Moreover, the rulers of the State themselves

---

50. The proximity of the British power in the neighbouring Punjab after 1846 made it very necessary for the State and its ruler to reorganize the entire army. D.K. Palit, *Jammu and Kashmir Arms*, pp. 50-55.
51. These were those of Thakur Kartar Singh of Jammu, Pandit Premnath Dhar of Karan Nagar, Raja Sahib Pandit Sham Sunder Lal Dhar, Raja Rajwali Khan of Zachaldar and Khawaja (Peer) Salam Shah of Jamia Masjid, Srinagar.
52. "Since British interest and influence in the northern reaches of India had grown to such large proportions in later part of 19th century, British officers and men had involved in undertakings which would otherwise have been solely the officers of Jammu and Kashmir State - and reciprocally J&K forces more and more frequently fromed a part of British endeavours...." D.K. Palit, *op.cit.*, p. 73-74, 86.

would scarcely want the army officials retain *jagirs* lest they strengthen their position and become a danger to the rulers.

Muafidars: Besides *jagir* grants, which were connected with the military or non-military services, there were the *muafi* grants which involved the remission of revenue. The practice of granting large tracts of land, both irrigated and unirrigated, as revenue free continued from ancient times down to the Dogra period.[53]

During the Muslim rule in India it was customary to grant land to Sayyids, Sheikhs and other non-Muslim subjects by way of *Madad-i-Maash* grants.[54] Even the Sikh rulers continued this practice of granting lands as *Madad-i-Maash to Muslims and Hindus.*[55]

---

53. The *term muafi* implies exemption from land revenue. This institution of *muafi* grants is also of an ancient standing in Kashmir. We have evidence to show that ancient rulers of Kashmir endowed revenue free land grants *(Agraharas)* to the charitable or religious institutions or personages. *Agrahara* as used by Kalhana meant a piece of land, the revenue of which was assigned to an individual or an institution for maintenance of sacred shrines. Kalhana's *Kajatarangini*, Eng. tr. Vol.I, 87-100, 121-175, 307, 340, 341 and 355.
   Among others M.A. Stein also mentions the fact that the custom of bestowing rent-free lands continued during Muslim and Sikh period, *Ibid.*, pp. 15-16, also n. 87.
54. Mir Ahmad, *Dastural Amal-i-Kashmir*, Per.Ms. ff. 215. Indu Banga, *Agrarian System of Sikhs*, pp.148-153. For details see B.N. Goswamy and J.S. Grewal, *Mughals and the Jogis of Jakhabar* pp. 17-46, 47-188, See also Athar Ali, *Mughal Nobility under Aurangzeb*, pp. 98-99. *Madad-i-maash* was land granted for subsistence to charitable institutions and religious persons. Another such revenue free grant came to be known as *Altamgha* -a grant by the royal stamp *(Tamgha)* the term *Altamgha* denoted a grant which was permanent and could not be resumed "except in case of misconduct". Baden Powell, *op.cit.*, pp. 530-31.
55. In fact Mir Ahmad has refered to thousands of muslim grantees of all categories. Mir Ahmad, *op.cit.*, ff. 184a, 206b, 207b, 208-9, 283a: also see ff. 326a-341b.

During the Dogra period as usual the *muafi* grants to Kashmiri Brahmans and Sayyid families remained intact. These families held this property under the pretext of institutions (temples, mosques and mathas etc.) ownership. The religious and charitable aspects of this phenomenon at times gave rise to quite a few problems in land relations. During the period under study many of these temple pandits and Sayyids joined the State services; still like absentee land lords, continued to receive the produce of these lands and the rights of the peasants who cultivated these lands were not determined. In course of time the practice of granting rent free lands to people in institution was abused even by ministers and provincial governors, who in order to avoid payment of revenue due to the State from them got their lands enlisted in the *Dharmarth* allotments.[56]

However, during the Dogra period *Muafis* were of two kinds one was religious and the other non-religious. In religious *muafi* one-third of the amount of land revenue assigned was received by the *muafidar* in cash and two-thirds in kind. The non-religious *muafis* were granted to persons for construction works of public use like bridges, wells etc.[57] In 1848 A.D. Vansagnew wrote to John Lawrence that the land revenue of Rs. 84,375 was assigned to the free grants held by religious personages and other learned men in the Persian, Arabic and Sanskrit language.[58]

---

56. One such example is of Dewan Badrinath who gradually got his *chak* enlisted as *Muafi* and made huge sums of money, A. Wingate, *op.cit*.p., 64.
57. *Karvai-Jalsa Council Aliya Jammu-va-Kashmir*, for the year 1898-1900. In case of non-religious *muafis* the whole of assigned land revenue was received either in cash or partly in cash and partly in kind. See R.C. Raina, "*Land Reforms*" *Kashmir* Vol. 2, No. 25-26, 16th December, 1952.
58. For. Dept. Sec. 31 March 1848, File Nos. 60-77, N.A..I.

The *muafi* grants were frequently hereditary in nature;[59] indeed, some of the *muafi* lands still remain attached to temples and *Mathas*.

Chakdars: Next in the hierarchy of the revenue assignees of Kashmir stood the *chakdars*. Although they were also a privileged class they stood quite low in comparison to the *jagirdars*. It was in 1862 when the State felt the need to get more and more waste lands under cultivation, it decided to grant pieces of land called chaks out of such waste land.[60] In the first instance grants called *chaks* were made for some ten years on condition that the wastelands should be brought under cultivation and only those should be employed to carry out cultivation who were not already cultivators in the lands of *jagirdars* or some other revenue assignee.[61] Some terms and conditions were laid down for these chakdars (holders of chaks) *i.e.*,

(*i*) that all rules of the State were to be obeyed;

(*ii*) that all rules were not included within the specific sanction;

(*iii*) that the lands would not be abandoned when the period of concessional rates had expired without paying for the period of possession at full rates;

(*iv*) that the holder must be loyal to the State and true to the caste;

(*v*) that if the State sanctioned sale, the purchasers would be similarly bound;

(*vi*) that the assessment would be levied whether the land was cultivated or not.[62]

---

59. *Jammu and Kashmir State Council Proceedings*, 26th Oct. 1904, p. 14, Jammu Archives.
60. A. Wingate, *op.cit.*, pp. 60-62. In fact these *chaks* were mostly allotted to the revenue officials and other favourites of the ruling family.
61. *Ibid.*
62. *Ibid.*, pp. 60-64.

These *chaks* were granted to the State employees in lieu of their services. They were entitled to hold possession of *chak* and to take away its agricultural produce so long as they paid State dues on land in due time.[63]

The *chakdars* entitled, free of charge, to use all the ordinary brushes and brushwood removed by them in cleaning the land for cultivation. But they were not entitled to trees on the land allotted to them without any payment.[64] Every *chakdar* was given a concession, *i.e.*, a fixed price that he had to pay for the purchase of any tree; it was to be paid by him in instalments, not exceeding five years from the date of the lease.[65] These *chakdars* were liable for payment, through *lambardar* of all State dues, according to the instalments fixed for the payment of land revenue in tracts in which the *chak* was situated.[66] If at all any *chakdar* failed to pay the instalment by due date, he was liable to be treated as defaulter under the law in force for realizing land revenue.[67] In case of *chakdars* who cultivated no part of land with their own hands the State demand was subject to reduction of 12½ per cent of revenue but not of the cesses assessed thereon.[68]

---

63. *Ibid.* See also *Rules regarding grant of waste land for cultivation as sanctioned by His Highness the Maharaja Sahib Bahadur*, Jammu, 1917, Jammu Archives.
64. *Ibid.*
65. *Ibid.*
66. *Ibid.*
67. However, this law came into force after the commencement of land settlements made by W.R. Lawrence A. Wingate, *op.cit.*, pp. 62-68. See also *Rules Regarding the Waste Land*, *op.cit.*, Jammu Archives.
68 This indeed was the ususal case. No *chakdar* cultivated the land with his own hands because mostly they lived in cities and used to visit *chak* generally at the time of harvest. As a result they came to be known as absentee landlords. See *A Review of the working of land reforms with special reference to Big landed Estates abolition act in Jammu and Kashmir*, Jammu, 1952.

The other obligations imposed upon these *chakdars* after the land settlement of 1889 were that they were asked to use due diligence in bringing the land under cultivation not less than 80 per cent of the total area granted within a period of 10 years from the date on which he received possession. The land allotted to a *chakdar* could in no condition be leased out for grazing of grass cutting instead of bringing it under cultivation.[69] He was entitled to transfer his right as such by sale, mortgage, gift or otherwise. He was also permitted on application to the *wazir wazarat* to have the name of any person closely related to him added on as co-sharer with himself, provided that the person was a subject of the State.[70] The *chakdar* after receiving possession of land and on fulfilment of the conditions of the grant received permanent right as an *assami* or occupancy tenant, he had thereafter the same rights and was subjected to the same liabilities as the other *assami* or occupancy tenants had in that area.[71] No *chakdar* could be ejected by the State within a period of twenty years, from the date of his lease otherwise than for failure to comply with the condition of his lease.[72] In case of eviction he was entitled to payment by the State of compensation for improvement to be fixed by the Governor in accordance with the law regulating compensation payable by landlords to tenants on ejectment. It was further laid down in the obligations imposed on these *chakdars* that if a *chakdar* to whom an *assami* right or permanent status had been granted, refused or without sufficient reason neglected to take up an area which was granted to him or if he withdrew his application at any stage after the measurement

---

69. *Rules regarding grant of waste land for cultivation as sanctioned by His Highness the Maharaja Gulsb Bahadur*, Jammu, 1917, Jammu Archives.
70. *Ibid.*
71. *Ibid.*
72. *Ibid.*

had commenced he was liable under the order of Governor for *Harjana* (cash penalty) at the rate of two annas per *kanal* to cover the cost of measurement.[73]

These *chaks* were of different kinds but the obligations or terms and conditions laid down were the same for all. From 1879 A.D. another class of landlords was created by granting *Mukarraree chaks* and *Ishtihari chaks*.[74] The terms and conditions for all these *chaks* were the same but the assessment for *Ishtihari chaks* was usually lighter than those of *Mukarraree chaks*.[75]

TABLE 6

The following table gives the rate of assessment on both.[76]

Year	*Rate of assessment for Dry land*			*Rate of assessment for Wet land*		
	Rs.	*annas*	*pies*	*Rs.*	*annas*	*pies*
1st	3	-	-	6	-	-
2nd	6	-	-	12	-	-
3rd	6	-	-	12	-	-

(Contd. on next page)

73. *Ibid.*
74. Besides *Mukarraree and Ishtiharee chaks* the other kinds of *chaks* were those of *zar-niasi, Ahalikaree, Hanudee,* the information regarding them is extremely scant. The *pattas* concerning the grant of *Mukarraree chaks* generally date from 1870 A.D. but no one paid any special attention to them because what the landlodrs desired was the means of occupying or obtaining land, they knew how to manipulate it. For instance during the famine of 1877 when most of the peasants had left their lands and had gone to the Punjab, the landlords got the opportunity for entering upon new lands temporarily left uncultivated and when the peasants returned from the Punjab they found themselves ousted. Generally land grants were made under the general order of *Dewan* and *Wazir-Wazarat* under their own signatures. A. Wingate, *op.cit.*, pp. 64-67.
75. *Mukarrarees* were a class of land holders, who were in receipt of fixed cash grants from the State either as a reward for their services to the State or as a charity. M.M.A. Beg, "Land Reforms in Jammu and Kashmir." *Main Stream*, New Delhi, 14th Annual Number, 1976, pp. 27-29.
76. A. Wingate, *op.cit.*, pp. 60-63.

(Contd. from previous page)

For *Ishtihari chak* the assessment was as follows:

1st		Free			Free	
2nd	0	10	-	1	-	-
3rd	1	-	-	2	-	-
4th	2	-	-	3	-	-
5th	2	-	-	4	-	-
6th	3	-	-	5	-	-
7th	4	-	-	6	-	-
8th	5	-	-	7	-	-
9th	6	-	-	8	-	-
					Rate of Assessment: per two acres	

Those in possession of *Ahalikaree chaks* got land in lieu of wages and on lump sum as will be clear from the following table.[77]

Year	*Amount in Rs.*
1st	Free of assessment
2nd	25
3rd	50
4th	75
5th	100
6th	125
7th	175
8th	250
9th	350
10th	500
from 11th	550

But the holders of all these *chaks* never observed the rules and regulations, they treated the orders of Durbar as mere formalities and exploited the peasant through rack renting and arbitrary and often forcible ejectment of tenants. They appropriated the major portion of the produce and hardly spent any money to improve the lands.

77. *Ibid.*, p. 63.

To quote Lawrence: "This was a common incident in Kashmir village. A pandit obtained a grant of waste land in village but neglected to cultivate it. The State then insisted on village to pay the assessment fixed on by Government. The *chakdar* did not cultivate it; the village was called upon to do so."[78]

The *chakdars* occupied much of the uncultivated land and included cultivable lands in their *chaks*. They evaded the payment of revenue and held even lands in excess.[79] We can cite a number of cases in which the *chakdars* held lands in excess of the grant by illegal means.

Dewan Badrinath got a grant of deserted government garden and with it was included some land he had bought from a women who appears to have been resourceless. For this land Dewan Badrinath was to pay Rs. 48 per annum. A few years later he bought some more land for Rs. 100 which he included in his *chak* and then being governor of Kashmir, he never paid even the usual revenue of Rs. 48 on the whole land which measured nearly 8 *kharwars* and 32 acres. As if it were not enough the Dewan gradually tried to convert it into *muafi* lands which was assessment-free.[80]

In another case a Pandit got a *chak* for ten *kharwars* of land but he modestly took possession of 9½ *kharwars* and held it for Rs. 1 for wet land and annas 8 for dry land per *kharwar* for 10 years. In 1873 Wazir Punoo doubled the assessment and after enquiry in 1877 it was found that the Pandit held six *kharwars* and eight *traks* more than he ought

---

78. In fact after the end of 19th century these *chakdars* who were mostly urban Hindu families, became an important force to reckon with. See Report by W.R. Lawrence, position of Cultivating classes in Kashmir, N.A.I., *Foreign Department, Secret, Feb. 1890*.

79. *Ibid.*

80. A. Wingate, *op.cit.*, pp. 63-64.

to have but he successfully resisted any increase in his assessment.[81]

These *chakdars* invented new devices of adding to their estates. Soon after taking possession of *chaks* they immediately ousted and expelled all the old cultivators in order to destory any proof of land having been cultivated when they entered upon it.[82] This would enable them to claim exemption from assessment for some time. Secondly they would extend their possession to every bit of land in the neighbourhood they could lay hands on.[83] A Tehsildar cast his eye upon a fine village within his charge, close to Srinagar. There were six or seven *kharwars* of land fallow and waste which supplied a pretext for developing the country and improving the revenue by applying for *chak.* He had good influence at headquarters, and his friend the Dewan about five years earlier gave him a *Mukarraree patta* for twenty *kharwars* of land at the rate of Rs. 12 for wet and Rs. 6 for dry land. But the Tehsildar took care to get it inserted that all lands were dry. He paid Rs. 150 only and was in possession of 29 *kharwars* of land of which 20¾ were irrigated and could produce a good *shali* crop."[84]

If a peasant died leaving his wife and children behind, the neighbouring *chakdar* was very alert in taking possession of his land under an agreement which would make him answerable for the revenue on the condition that the land would be restored to the family when the children

---

81. *Ibid.* See *Report of W.R. Lawrence regarding the Position of Cultivating classes in Kashmir, Feb., 1890,* N.A.I. See also *Foreign Deptt. Secretariate,* E. File No. 295-326.
82. A. Wingate, *op.cit.,* pp. 63-64.
83. *Ibid.*
84. A. Wingate, *op.cit.,* p. 64. Here it becomes clear that to be in the State Service and particularly in the revenue Department was a good fortune where the officials had ample chances of making wealth by resorting to fraudulent practices.

grew up. Inevitably, not in all cases was the land thus restored. Some times these *chakdars* picked up a quarrel about their boundary and made an addition of a few *kharwars* of land to their estate. When during the last years of Maharaja Ranbir Singh's reign and the early years of Maharaja Pratap Singh it became known to all the revenue assignees and grantees that the land settlement was to commence very soon and it had become less difficult for all the *chakdars* to obtain lands they resorted to other practices of occupying *chaks*. They used to extract pledge from the villagers that such and such a village, in which they were interested had been the property of such and such a pandit and pretended that somehow the possession had been lost, and then the villagers recognized him as proprietor and agreed that he shall pay the assessment.[85] At times deeds of sale were executed for a very meagre amount which was never paid.[86]

With the commencement of regular land settlement in 1889, the State attempted an enquiry and laid down that the authority granting the land should first be examined. With regard to the land held in excess by the *chakdars* possession was to be recognized unless on report of the settlement the excess was resumed.[87]

As to the tenure of land, with regard to the peasants under *chakdars* it was laid down that the settlement officer should be entrusted with full powers to decide which cultivators should have the right of occupancy under *chakdars* and they was usually given such right of occupancy in

---

85. Mr. Wingate states that in one Tehsil villages were made over to influential officials like *Wazir Wazarat*, Secretaries and the governor and none of them used to pay the revenue consequently great loss was registered in State finances. *Ibid.*, p. 64.
86. *Rules regarding grant of State waste land for Cultivation.*
87. *Ibid.*

respect of lands reasonably believed to have been cultivated land, whether temporarily follow or not.[88]

With regard to the assessment of *chakdars chak* the Durbar decided with the advice of Mr. Wingate that grant of possession to cultivate waste lands at reduced rates for a specific period did not confer upon any grantee any privileges in respect of assessment after the term of years specified elapsed and the settlement was therefore free to impose the same assessment upon any *chakdar* as upon any peasant and *patta* since the commencement was declared useless.[89]

Each *chak* was to be assessed in an ordinary way at its full value and that after a consideration of how and why land was obtained , the expenditure attendant on bringing it under cultivation, the treatment of peasants the amount hitherto be paid as compared with the land taken possession of and other such points, the settlement officer was asked to seek the sanction of Durbar. For this he was asked to make such reduction as may seem fair to him on full assessment and this reduced assessment was to be demanded during the term or period of settlement.[90]

---

88. *Ibid*. See also Wingate, *op.cit.*, pp. 68-69.
89. *Ain Pratap Code Part II*. Ain No. 5 Jammu Archives. See also *Rules regarding grant of State Waste land for Cultivation*.
    Pandit Bhag Ram, *Report on Administration of Jammu-va-Kashmir*, 1889-90. pp. 37-43.
    See also *Big Landed estates abolition Act*, XVII of S. 2007, Jammu, 1953.
90. The reasons for this reduction were that almost all revenue officials were in receipt of *chaks*, so the Durbar did not deem it just, not politic, on their part to force out all *chakdars;* and secondly if the full assessment was to be levied there was no room for middlemen.
    Karvai-Jalsa Council Aliya for the year 1889-90. (See portion on Mahkama-Mal)

5
Condition of Peasantry

To analyse the condition of peasantry of a particular region, ideally very many aspects should be examined in detail, *viz.*, the size of land holding per household, the nature and extent of production, the technology and the social organization of labour use, stratification within the peasantry and the relationship among various social classes.[1] In the case of Kashmir, the sources provide us with very little information on many of these aspects. On the basis of such information as is available only broad distinctions amongst different ranks of the peasantry can be attempted such as the landless agricultural labourer, the tenant and the peasant proprietor.

The condition of peasantry taken as a whole had already reached a low ebb when Maharaja Gulab Singh took over the administration in 1845 A.D.[2]

---

1. In studying the rural society of Kashmir, one of most persistent weaknesses is the difficulty to distinguish between various social classes in the agrarian class structure in which they arise and the different strata to which they belong. This difficulty is rooted in the lack of sources, relevant to rural property and class structure. As a result the peasantry of Kashmir has often been treated as an undifferentiated group.
2. Until the annexation of the Punjab by the British in 1846, Kashmir

(Contd. on next page)

Lawrence in a letter to Currie wrote, "the people seem in a wretched state of poverty. It will be years and years before this country can recover its prosperity. It will be pleasant land for a man to dwell in."[3]

As far as the material life of the peasantry was concerned coarse rice and *sag* constituted their usual food.[4] Where little paddy was grown people depended on maize.[5] Even wheat was grown here but the cakes of bread prepared out of wheat flour were taken with tea and not for the chief meals. The poor peasants subsisted on fruits and vegetables.[6] Although milk was abundant but the peasants

---

(Contd. from previous page)

had been a part of that State. But with the conclusion of treaty of Amritsar between Maharaja Gulab Singh and the British in 1846 A.D. Jammu and Kashmir with certain adjustment of frontiers were constituted into the State of Jammu and Kashmir and handed over the Maharaja Gulab Singh. Though political future of Jammu, Kashmir and the Frontier Territories was settled, their economic conditions remained more or less the same. Whereas the Punjab began to register some progress as a result of ameliorative measures of the British Government the State of Jammu and Kashmir did not receive any settled advantage. Hence the condition of the newly founded State was deplorable. S.M. Rai, *Partition of Punjab*, New York, 1965, p. 22. See also Elzabeth Whitecomb, *Agrarian conditions in Northern India*, Delhi 1971, Vol. I, pp.64-75.

3. The letter from H.M. Lawrence to Gurrie. See No. 1240-41 Dec. 8, 1846, Jammu Archives.
4. The term *sag* implies green vegetable leaves cooked in every Kashmiri house almost everyday. W. Wakefield, *op.cit.*, p. 136.
5. Hargopal Koul Khasta, *Guldasta-i-Kashmir*, p. 75. M.D. Fauq, *Rahnuma-i-Kashmir*, pp. 63-64.
6. Ganeshi Lal,. *Sayahatnama*, p. 34. Vegetables and fruits did not comprise the staple food of Kashmiri peasant and the sense that fruit was a constituent of rich diet was not present. Its supply being abundant there was practically no commercial demand for fruit. In the absence of quick and inadequate means of communication and transport with the outside world, a perishable commodity like fruit could not be carried over long distances. Therefore it commanded no price. *Statement of moral and material progress* (1888-89) J.A., p. 168.

consumed very small part of it. Out of the major share *ghee* was made and handed over to the money lender.[7] Fedrick Drew rightly remarks, "The country people are but poorly off. I think indeed, that they get a fair meal, but they can afford little beyond their simple daily food, and are unable to provide against a rainy day, when a bad years comes, as though not often does sometimes happen, they are put to great straits and will perhaps leave the country in number for the isolation of the place 16 such that it is exceedingly difficult for any great importation of corn to be made to redress the failure of the harvest." [8]

The vegetables in regular consumption were knol Khol, turnips, pumpkins, radish and brinjal.[9] The poor peasants living near the Wular lake or on its banks subsisted on *Singharas*. Hasan says:

"مفلوک تنگدستان مردم بجز بادر علاقه بانڈی پور و حاجن و سوپور
بلکه در تمام علاقه پائین آبش کرده می خورند" 1

"The poor people of Bandipore, Hajan and sopore rather the entire poor population of lower region below these subsisted on boiled *singharas* (waternuts)."[10]

Though salt and tea were costly items the consumption of salt was higher because the Kashmiri peasant preferred

---

7. Wreford, *Census*, 1941, XXII, p. 19.
8. F. Drew, *Jammu & Kashmir Territories*, London, 1875, p. 176.
9. M.D. Fauq, *op.cit.*, pp. 61-66.
10. Hassan, *op.cit.*, Vol. I, p. 186.

salty vegetables and took salty tea twice or thrice a day. Mutton was beyond the access of this section of population even on festive occasions.

The peasants of Kashmir could hardly afford utensils other than those of clay. They lived in simple huts, the roofs of which were covered with straw and rice husk: straw was considered best for it.[11] Moorcraft says, "The houses were unplastered and badly constructed with broken doors. Near the forests the roofs were made of wooden singhals and the houses were real log huts, the wall being made of whole logs laid one upon the other, like the cottages of Russian peasantry."[12] There was no furniture in their houses and no bed steads existed; instead at night a cloth was spread on the ground for each person and a blanket to cover him. In some areas the peasants used to sleep on mats only.[13]

Oil was used for lighting purposes and in higher villages, use was made of torches of pine wood. Fire was used in winter, Lawrence says, "Kangar (firepot) forms an important part of the Kashmiris life."[14]

At the lowest rung of the peasantry was the agricultural wage labourer. His condition was truly dismal. He was given one meal and six seers of unhusked rice a day. After feeding his family he could save one anna a day or two

---

11. David Ross, *Land of Five Rivers and Sind*, p. 105.
    T. Biscoe, *Kashmir in Sunlight and Shade*, London, p. 87.
    W. Wakefield, *op.cit.*, p. 265. E.F. Knight, *op.cit.*, pp.76-77, Wreford, *op.cit.*, p. 37.
12. Moorcraft, as cited in Lawrence, *Valley*, p. 249.
13. E.F. Knight, *op.cit.*, pp. 76-77. Charles Girdlestone, *op.cit.*, pp. 155-62.
14. *Ibid.* (Kangri) Portable brazier is an interesting feature of the life of Kashmiris. Every Kashmiri makes use of it during winter. They cannot afford to part with it at least from four to five months in a year. It becomes constant companion of Kashmiris.

rupees a month on disposing of his surplus rice.[15] It is to be noted that this agricultural wage labourer was engaged in agricultural pursuit only for a specific period not exceeding five months a year. Therefore, this section of labourers migrated to the plains during winter months to earn their sustenance.[16] Very few, if any among this section supplemented their income at home by taking to weaving of woolen blankets and baskets while staying at home.[17]

Another section of the peasants comprised the tenants, who worked on the lands of the *jagirdars, chakdars* and *muafidars*. This class of landed aristrocracy rented out their lands to the tenants and shared the crops annually with them.[18] The tenancy system was very wide-spread in Kashmir.

Partly the administrative system of the period compelled large sections of the peasants to give up cultivation and work as tenants, as we shall discuss below. Besides, widespread existence of parasitic landlordism also encouraged tenancy system.[19] These rented holdings varied greatly in size.[20] Though these tenants had to pay half the produce in rent but they were never free from rendering other obligations in the form of produce and labour.

---

15. Vigne, *Travels*, Vol. II., p. 120.
    Among the agricultural labourers there were two categories one of those who new the cultivation and the other was those of unskilled labourers in general.
16. Some of them used to carry loads to the Punjab and also worked as porters in Lahore to earn their living. Lawrence, *Valley*, p. 253.
17. Charles Girdlestone, *Memorandum of Kashmir*, p. 30. Since the basket makers job was not a regular opening the agricultural workers had to move out of his village and find for himself the job of preparing the *Kangris* (fire-pots etc.).
18. A. Wingate, *op.cit.*, pp. 60-71.
19. *Ibid.* See also *Karvai-Jalsa-Council Aliya,* for the year 1898-1900. A.D. Srinagar Archives.
20. A. Wingate, *op.cit.*, pp. 60-71.

In Kashmir this tenancy appears to have served a useful function when the land owning class had no interest in maximizing agricultural production but merely wanted to maximize its own surplus. Because leasing out land enable a landlord to collect rent without any effort on their part, freed him from tedious choice of supervising a hired labour force, allowed him to reap the surplus product quietly and unostentatiously.[21] Hence the position of these tenants was deplorable. The landowner shifted much of the risk of the crop failure consequently the income of the tenant became variable. The landowners never provided inputs to the tenants. These tenants usually did not possess heritable rights and landowners could reoccupy the property at will. Due to poverty, the tenant was forced to lease land on whatever terms was available to him to feed his family. They had to carry or bear the charges of transporting the share of produce to their lords place and to enable them to live as absentee landlords.[22] In some cases these tenants were of long standing on the estate but in many cases they were migratory persons who could move freely and change their masters. They were, however, entirely unprotected by law. Their share of rent could be enhanced without any adequate notice. They could be evicted any time for default in the payment of rent or any other obligatory service. Their eviction too was not regulated by any procedure framed for their protection.[23]

---

21. In the wake of heavy pressure of land, the practice landlord could take advantage of the competition for land by extracting onerous rents from the tenant and it was also a means of hiring labour at below subsistence wages. *Karvai-Jalsa-Council-Aliya,* 1898-1900, Srinagar Archives.
22. *The Big Landed Estates Abolition Act No. XVII,* Jammu, 1953.
23. *Patta granted to Pandit Raja Kak Dhar regarding grant of Jagir in Hamal Ilaqa,* 1866, Srinagar Archives. See for details. A. Wingate, *op.cit.,* pp. 60-67 and M.M.A. Beg, *Zara-i-Islahat,* pp. 8-9.

Next comes the peasant proprietor about whose rights in land a lot of confusion has been created by the then corrupt officials.[24] They deprived the peasants of their proprietory rights through fraudulent practices some of which have been described graphically by Mr. Wingate: "to please the Durbar and allay apprehension, every official glibly agrees that land belongs to His Highness. Accordingly deeds of sale and agreements generally refer to the right possessed by the *zamindars*, with a judicious mixture of words denoting ownership and property. These documents are duly registered by the courts. Upon them petitions are based and a good deal of correspondence ensures, and finally the Durbar passes orders and so endorses the whole. Take an instance, the son of an influential official took a contract in the old days for two villages. in 1880 the *khewat* (cash assessment) was made with him. Next year he petitioned to the *Wazir Wazarat*

---

24. The question of ownership of land is a legal question with very little socio-economic content in the medieval context, as has been argued by Harbans Mukhia in "Was there Feudalism in Indian History?", Presidential Address, Medieval India Section, India History Congress, Fortieth Session, Waltair, 1979. Irfan Habib on the basis of thoroughgoing examination of the evidence has very rightly disputed the assertion of foreign travellers and some scholars that land belonged to the king. The tradition of agrarian system or landholdings was quite contrary to the statement made out by these travellers and scholars. Payment of land tax should not be taken to mean that land belonged to ruler. Irfan Habib, *Agrarian System of Mughal India*, pp. 111-13. Other eminent historians like B.R. Grover have also argued in favour of peasant ownership of land, see his "Nature of Land-Rights in Mughal India," I.E.S.H.R., Vol. I., No. 1, 1963, pp. 2-5 and "Nature of Dehat-i-Taaluqa (Zamindari villages) and the evolution of the Taaluqdari system during the Mughal Age, "I.E.S.H.R, Vol. II, No. 2 & 3 1965, pp. 261-62. In case of Kashmir during the period of our study officials supported the view that the ownership vested with the king and not the peasant.

that he was being hindered paying the revenue of the village which are his property. Then *Wazir Wazarat* submits the case for orders and an endorsement was written across a corner that petitioner was allowed to pay the revenue of the villages which are his *milkiat* and *zamindari*.[25]"

Generally the sale and mortgage of the land was not disallowed. Besides *karvais* provide us with frequent references to the sale and mortgage of land. The disappearance of the proprietorship in land took place because of some economic problems like *begar* (corvee) and the heavy tax burden.[26] It was as a result of such practices that the holdings of the peasant proprietors were transferred to revenue officials.[27]

Though the peasant proprietors paid land revenue, they were not free from interference on the part of the State, at the time of reaping and storing of the grains.[28] This left them with little incentive to improve productivity of their land.

The other allied pursuit apart from cultivation which the peasant practised was bee-keeping. Honey was

---

25. A. Wingate, *op.cit.*, p. 65. It is as a result of this confusion that both the travellers and the native writers stated that the ruler was the owner of land and not the peasant.
26. When peasants were taken away from their lands to render corvee, on their return they often found themselves landless. Besides when the maximum produce of the peasant proprietors was snatched away by the revenue officials under various heads he left the field and recruited himself as wage labourer but at times when he came back after some time he found himself ousted and his holding was entered by officials against their own names, A. Wingate, *op.cit.*,pp. 60-64.
27. *For Dept. Sec.C. March 31, 1848. Files Nos. 66-70*, N.A.I.
28. Mirza, Saif-ud-Din, *Akhbarat*, Vol. I, f. 44. See also H.M. Lawrence, *Transfer of Govt. to Maharaja Gulab Singh*, Section C., Jan. 1848, File Nos. 33-44, J.A.

produced not only for consumption but also for sale. However, the earnings from this were negligible and too meagre to substantially add to low returns from their holdings.[29] It was this class of peasants who took to weaving of blankets and baskets during the off season.[30] The migration of this class of peasants was not a taboo and a few of these, particularly those oppressed by the money-lenders' exacting demands left their homes during winter months to earn their livelihood.[31] In undertaking these subsidiary crafts the peasants usually suffered from the greed and rapacity of the middlemen. Wazir Ganganath very rightly remarks, "Substantial gains could accrue to the cultivator only where these crafts were organized on cooperative basis, thus eliminating the middlemen and were sufficiently accessible to marketing centres."[32]

---

29. James Korbel who visited Kashmir in the first half of the 20th century says that about 60 per cent of the peasants had the holdings of about 16 kanals (two acres) each. Their net annual income was Rs. 10-10-3, per head. The rest of the peasantry was without land. Even as late as 1944-45 the per capita income of the peasant did not exceed eleven rupees. J.Korbel, *Danger in Kashmir,* Srinagar, 1954, p. 16.
30. Since the basket making was not a regular opening during the off season the peasants of Kashmir used to weave home spun cotton and wool for their domestic use but their methods were primitive and looms were also of an ancient type. Lawrence, *Valley*, pp. 310-11. *A note on Jammu and Kashmir State*, p. 36. See also Charles Girdlestone, *op.cit.*, p. 30.
31. A.L. Admas, *Wanderings of a naturalist in India*, Edinburg, 1867. See also Wreford, *Census of India*, 1941, Vol.XXII, p.8.
32. These subsidiary crafts included manufacturing of *Pattu* (woolen cloth) cloth weaving, needlework, oil pressing, pottery, epiculture, poultry keeping, silkworm rearing. There were, besides, occupations of horticulture and collection of medicinal herbs. Wazir Ganganath, *Report on Jammu & Kashmir State*, 1943. (type-script) Jammu Archives, p. 69.

Nature too occasionally took its toll of peasant lives. In 1848, owing to heavy rainfall the peasants of Kashmir suffered from different diseases in large numbers so much so that every family lost a few of its members to the epidemic. The same year saw the famine as a result of which a huge cattle wealth of the peasant was destroyed for want of grass and fodder.[33] Mirza Saif-ud-Din says that as a result of excessive heat in the preceding seasons and the drought the soil became so hard that it became difficult for the peasant to plough and to lay seeds; then suddenly it rained so heavily that fields were lost in flood.[34]

In 1852 there prevailed general scarcity of food grains and the peasants had to depend on barley and many of them left the country.[35] In 1856 the peasants distress was intensified by the terrible earthquake coupled with the failure of the season's rains, so that all lands were sown with maize or other coarse cereals for avoiding loss in the revenue and to fall back upon. In 1877 also the peasants had to face a very harsh situation, the crops were destroyed by unusual rains and more than half of the crop was lost, consequently a large section of the population died.[36]

This was followed by a terrible femine of 1879 which caused a further loss of men and material.[37]

---

33. Mirza, *op.cit.*, Vol. I, ff. 52-53..
34. *Ibid.*, Vol. I, ff. 52-53.
35. *Ibid.*, Vol.V, ff. 71-72.
36. Younghusband, *Kashmir*, pp.180-81, G.C. Bruce, *op.cit.*, p. 39. See for details Lawrence, *Valley*, p. 213. This calamity dislocated the peasantry, the charity houses were opened at different places. Please see the table at p. 11.
37. Even during this period the State did not relax its control over the peasantry. Instead the State continued to leave no surplus grain with peasants. Everything was taken from them and stored in State Stores at Srinagar. Lawrence, *Valley*, p. 217.

TABLE 7

Table giving detail of charity houses and the expenditure incurred therein for feeding the people who were tormented with famine in 1877[38].

S. No.	Name of Wazarat	No. of charity houses estab-lished	No. of people fed	Quantity of grains distri-buted		Expenses incurred		Misce-lleneous expenses	
				Mmds.	*Seers*	*Rs*	*annas*	*Rs*	*annas*
1.	Shahar-i-Khas	5	58,896	1178	–	2945	–	312	8
2.	Kamraj	3	60,261	1324	20	2948	12	155	13
3.	Patan	5	33,150	813	–	1657	8	85	10
4.	Shopian	5	31,787	1038	–	1095	–	123	5
5.	Anantnag	5	62,595	2032	10	3102	8	235	5
6.	Muzaffarabad	4	13,485	285	37	1181	8	929	9
7.	Grand Total	27	2,60,174	6671	27	12930	4	1842	2

38. *Majmu-i-Report Jammu, Kashmir and Tibet* 1877-78, pp. 18-19.

In 1885 the earthquake made its appearance and increased the suffering of the people by causing distress and starvation. The suffering has been described by Hasan in these words. "During Maharaja Ranbir Singh's time Kashmir was visited by earthquake which took heavy toll of men and material, accounting for 35,000 which included 20, 000 horses, 10,200 cows, 1,500 human lives."[39]

Again in 1893, Kashmir was visited by flood which cost the State Rs. 64,804 in land revenue alone, 35,426 acres under crops were submerged, 2,225 houses were wrecked and 329 cattle killed.[40]

Hence the peasantry of Kashmir appears to have been in constant state of agony. The frequency of these natural calamities gravely undermined the position of the peasant and he had no alternative but to rush to the money-lender.[41]

In favourable seasons too the peasant was hardly in a position to improve his lot. The State had a monopoly over

---

39. Hassan, *Tarikh-i-Hasan*, Vol. I, p. 471-72.

"در ایام مہاراجہ رنبیر سنگھ --- بہ وقوع زلزلہ حادثہ در کل
قلمرو کشمیر سی و پنج ہزار جاندار بے جان گشت از آن جملہ
مواشی بیست ہزار اسپان و گاوان دہ ہزار و از نوع انسان
ہزار و پانصد کس"

The number of 35000 is obviously a rough computation, for the details, given by Hassan add upto only 31,700.

40. Lawrence, *Valley*, p. 205.
41. The money lending system was known as *Wadhadari* (system under which the *khoja* traders, (village shop-keepers) and *Galladars* who by charging interest multiplied their profits and called it *Wadh*. The usual time for money lending in Kashmir was winter and summer season, Lawrence, *Valley*, p. 5. See also *Assessment Report of Pratap Singh Pora Tensil*, 1917, p. 45.

grain trade and it was not possible for the peasant to sell or obtain grains at reasonable prices.[42]

Owing to the lack of credit facilities on the part of the State, necessary for productive operations, the peasant was at the mercy of *Wadhdar* (money-lender). Whenever the peasant required loan for cattle the money-lender advanced it to him against the security of the crop whose value was assessed at lower rates than those prevailing in the market.[43] If the crops failed due to natural calamity and the peasant could not meet the quantity of crop contracted, the money-lender charged the residue of the crop at enhanced rates and a new contract took place. In this way a loan once contracted was seldom liquidated even for generations.[44]

On the other hand social customs dictated spending beyond ones means on occasions like wedding, birth, death etc. and the *wadhdar* was at hand to offer loan. Since the rate of interest was very high, once the peasant fell into the

---

42. During Maharaja Gulab Singh's reign in 1856 the State procured Shali from the peasants at the rate of one rupee and fourteen annas per *kharwar* and sold the same quantity for two rupees and twelve annas. Mir Saifullah, *Tarikhnama-Kashmir* (Per. Ms. 1806-66) Prof. Z.L. Jalla of Kashmir University has been kind enough to lend me this manuscript for consultation.
43. *Assessment Report of Pratap Singh Pora Tehsil, 1917,* p. 45. The following table is a clear example of the money-lenders device.

Name of grain	*Fixed rates of money-lender*			*Rates in the market*		
	Rs.	*an.*	*p.*	*Rs.*	*an.*	*p.*
Shali	1	8	0	1	12	0
Maize	1	8	0	1	12	0
Wheat	3	0	0	4	0	0
Til-gogulo (oilseed)	4	0	0	5	0	0

44. Dewan Krishan Lal, *op.cit.*, p. 20-22, Lawrence, *Valley*, p. 5.

hands of the money-lender, he remained for generations in the rigmarole of repayment of interest and debt with little hope of redemption.[45] Yet, the money-lender is seldom looked upon with bitterness, for he was the only source on which the peasant could fall back upon whatever his need.

Even as late as 1906, 60 per cent of the peasants were affected by this money-lending system. The average annual rate of interest was 81 per cent. The average land-holding in the valley was about four acres. With average debt rate at Rs 9-6-4 per acre, it amounted to Rs. 37-9-4 per holding and the annual interest on it came to Rs 13-2-5 at the minimum and Rs. 48-7-9 at the maximum exacted by the money-lender.[46]

Mr. H.W. Brailsford a prominent English journalist who visited Kashmir in the first half of twentieth century observed. "The peasants of Kashmir are sunk in unimaginable poverty. Their mud-huts contain hardly any trace of visible property, save a pot or jar. When I put my question in a typical village every house-hold was in debt and the usual rates of interest were 45 per cent."[47]

Another most hated institution for Kashmiri peasant was that of forced labour, *Begar* or corvee. The system had been developed in Kashmir by former rulers but it touched its height under the Dogra rulers.[48] Maharaja Gulab Singh introduced reforms regarding *Begar* but did not abolish it.

The peasants of Kashmir were often pressed into *Begar*

---

45. *Karvai-Jalsa-Council Aliya for the year 1898-1900*, Jammu Archives.
46. *Note on the Review of Six Tehsils of the Valley*, (published by Jammu & Kashmir Government), Jammu, p. 11.
47. H.W. Brailsford, "Kashmir Today through Foreign eyes", Bombay, 1948.
48. Kalhana states in *Rajatarangini* that Samkarvarman who ruled Kashmir from 833-902 A.D. is well known for his fiscal oppression. He levied fines on those villagers who did not carry their loads

(Contd. on next page)

at the time of sowing and reaping and made to work for several purposes. They were asked to carry loads of the British visitors to Kashmir, to construct *bandhs* and bridges, to cultivate the lands of revenue officers and also to carry rations to different army quarters. In 1848 *Wazir* Ratnu collected a good number of peasants, 1000 from pargana *Lal*, 500 from pargana *Pakh*, 20 from *mouza Pain* (Lower portion of the same pargana) 1000 peasants from *pargana Ich Nagam* for raising *bandhs*.[49] In 1847 the peasants of Kashmir were forcibly collected for cleaning the wool which had been collected by the revenue officials without any payment.[50]

P. Grevis observes, "The dreaded begar system of unpaid forced which was nothing less than slave hunting was reintroduced in the country. The State armed forces rounding up all the able bodied men sending them away for long periods to distant places to labour as coolies often never returned. The fields were tended by the old men and the old women as best as they could. The young women hide themselves under long wide *burqas* which cover them from the crown of their heads to their feet, whilst the boys suffered the same fate as their brothers had done hundreds of years before the corinth. Again thousands fled the

---

(Contd. from previous page)

voluntarily. The fines levied amounted to the value of the load. Kalhana, *Rajatarangini* (English tr. M.A. Stein, London, 1900, p. 209). Stein observed that suffering arising out of *Begar* continued till the construction of Gilgit road. *Ibid.*, Vol. II, p. 172-74. During the medieval times this oppressive practice remained in tact. Mughal emperors turned it into regular institution and the peasants were made use of for carrying the baggage of the visitors and armymen to Kashmir.

49. Mirza, *op.cit.*, Vol. I, f. 74.
50. *Ibid*, Vol. I., ff. 29, 62. The custom *begar* appears to have been not only forcible but at times unpaid also.

country this time they were muslims."[51] As a result of this custom the peasants of Kashmir had lost all attraction for home and started fleeing to other parts of the country leaving behind their family and children. During *chilas* compaign in 1851 Dewan Jowala Sahai ordered that one man from each peasant family should be collected for carrying ration, army equipment and other necessaries of life for soldiers deputed to the campaign.[52] Thus was an army of 30 thousand *begarees* collected which included peasants, non-agriculturists, boatmen and common people.[53]

Every year thousands of peasants were driven off from their lands to toil as carriers of burdens on the Gilgit road. In 1856, recruitment of two thousand load carriers was made from among the peasants of Kashmir to carry grains etc. to Gilgit campaign.[54] Enormous transport service was needed to supply the garrisons on the northern frontier with grain. The Kashmiri authorities were very careless about the lives of their unfortunate peasants, who were dragged from their homes and families for months together to starve on the Gilgit road.[55] "Gilgit is the name of terror throughout the State."[56] Hasan says, "In samvat 1937 *i.e.* 1880 the inhabitants of Gilgit demanded their ususal rights... revolted and a few of soldiers raided the fort *Sher-Qilla*. And when Maharaja Ranbir Singh heard this news he

---

51. P. Grevis, *This is Kashmir*, London, 1954, pp. 57-58.
52. Mirza, *op.cit.*, Vol. IV, ff. 61,78 and 84. For details see A.P. Nicholson, *Scrapes of Paper, India's broken Treaties, her princes and her problem*, London, 1930, pp. 100-102.
53. Mirza, *op.cit.*, Vol. IV, f. 84.
54. *Ibid.*, Vol. IX, ff. 43-50.
55. Hasan, *Tarikh-i-Hasan*, Vol. II, pp. 869-70. *Imperial Gazetteer of India*, Vol. IX, p. 78.
56. Lawrence, *Valley*, pp. 411-13.

sent three thousand soldiers. For transporting their language and food upto Hasura, peasants were brought to render forced labour (*begar*). In this operation many of the peasants lost their lives and thousands of rupees were given as bribes by the peasants to escape the forced labour."[57]

The system was highly discriminatory. The government officials and the peasants who worked on *khalsa* lands and *jagirs* and *chaks* of the influential officials and lands allotted to temples and *Mathas* were exempted from *Begar*.[58] Pandits, Peers and the urban people were also exempted from this dreaded custom.[59]

The peasants could hardly escape the clutches of the revenue officials. The system also encouraged large scale corruption by obtaining wood, grass, milch cows and sheep free of any cost. Besides the revenue officials cultivated their lands and built houses for their use with the unpaid labour of the peasant.[60] It also led to the destruction of proprietory rights of the peasants and reduced them to a

---

57. Hasan, *op.cit.*, pp. 869-70. The original text reads as follows:

"سنه ۱۹۳۷ ب --- دران اثنا ساکنان علاقهٔ گلگت با اصطلاح حقوق
معمولی خود که در دادن آن اهمال شده بود - شورش کرده چند کس از
سپاهیان شیر قلعه بقتل آوردند و باستماع این خبر مهاراجه برای
سرکوبی باغیان سه هزار سپاه مامور ساخت و بابت باربرداری
و رسانیدن غلات تا حصوره زمینداران به بیگاری بردند -
بسیاری از جان تلف شدند و هزاران مبلغ در مواخذه رشوه برای
گرفت و گذاشت بیگاریان از زمینداران گرفتند -

58. Lawrence, *Valley*, p. 412. The Silk rearers were also free from this forced labour, P. Grevis, *op.cit.*, p. 154.
59. E.F. Knight, *op.cit.*, p. 70. A. Wingate, *op.cit.*, p. 70. See also N.D. Nargis, *Tarikh-i-Dogra Desh* (Urdu), p. 425.
60. Lawrence, *Valley*, p.414. E.F. Knight, *op.cit.*, p. 69.

state close to serfdom.[61] Most of the *begar* was carried on in summer when the peasants were needed in their fields; thus the crops largely suffered in their absence. They were given only as much food as could sustain them. As a result of this their families too suffered in the absence of their bread-winner.[62] Sometimes these peasants would lose their lives during the course of their service in *begar* and it was then that their families would permanently become victims of hunger and starvation.[63]

These were the marked features of agrarian economy of Dogra rule and naturally had an adverse effect on the agrarian economy of the country. The oppressive system led to the depopulation of the peasants and in a way led to the growing migration of peasants. In order to avoid the brunt of *begar* the peasants sought refuge elsewhere, thus they had to flee from one village to another. This consequently led to the transference of the land from actual owners of the soil, to the powerful bureaucracy of Dogra rulers easily, for there are reports of some villages being sold by the peasants for a petty sum in order to earn exemption from *begar*.[64]

---

61. *Ibid.*, pp. 12-22. It is not be wondered at, therefore, that the peasants started fleeing to the Punjab. The villages of *Kajliban and Bhagtur* which were reduced from 15 to 6 and 150 to 30 respectively are clear examples of depopulation of villages. Maharaja Pratap Singh, *Diary*, pp. 20-22.
62. E.F. Knight, *op.cit.*, pp. 69-70. Political Dept. S.A.R., 1906, File No. 77 J.A. See also Pol. Dept., S.A.R., 1913, File No. 213, J.A.
63. Foreign Dept. Sec. E. December 1890, file Nos. 196-211, N.A.I. Foreign Dept. Sec. E. Feb. 1891, File Nos. 295-306, N.A.I. E.F. Knight, *op.cit.*, p. 70.
64. In one case three villages were sold to the *Hakim-i-Ala* (Governor of Kashmir) for miserly amounts giving an average of about Rs. 40 per village. V.R. Lawrence, *Valley*, p. 414. Because once a peasant rendered himself landless he could easily escape from *Begar* after making a move from his habitation to any other part of country.

Begar, however, was not unique to Kashmir. It was resorted to in the Punjab where it continued for good many years.[65] But in Kashmir the abuse rather than the use of *begar* was the real evil. As Lawrence very rightly remarks, "A man could sometimes hide his grain in secret pits (zusu) and could save enough food to keep him and his children alive till the fruits and vegetables came, but it was more difficult to hide himself when the officials were on the look-out for human carriage, and the Kashmir pressgang would watch and wait if a reluctant villager fled to the mountains. *Begar* means to the Kashmiris far more than imprisonment of labour, for under its comprehensive name every kind of demand for labour or property taken but not paid for by the officials was included."[66]

The position of the peasants was also undermined by numerous religious and social factors. The peasants of Kashmir, like their counterparts in other parts of the country, were deeply steeped in conservatism and tradition. The fatal hold that was exercised by Sayyids, Rishis, Babas and the Brahmans did not permit the peasant to make efforts for improving their lot.[67] They attributed all natural and man-made calamities to the curse of God.[68] This entire

---

65. Foreign Dept. File No. 15, 29th Jan. 1890, R.P. *Nisbets Letter to the Secretary to Govt. of India*, N.A.I.
66. W.R. Lawrence, *Valley*, p. 411.
67. Indeed, remedy for the prevalent deficiency of irrigation was sought by the peasants in the 'Supernatural' powers of the Sayyids and saints. This is understandable, in the absence of any institutional support to cultivation. *Ibid.*, pp. 215-17. G.T. Vigne, *Travels*, Vol. II, p. 171.
68. The droughts, earthquakes, cholera, famines and the cruality of rulers were all attributed to God. In order to get relief from these calamities, though temporarily, the peasants were made to part with their cattle-wealth and the surplus amount of produce, in the shape of offerings by these Sayyids and Saints. Charles Baron Hugel, *The Punjab and Kashmir*, Jammu, 1972, p. 90. Victor Jacqoue-Mont, *Letters from Indis*, London 1834, p. 328.

structure of backward agriculture, a highly exploitative ruling class and the cultural primitiveness pushed the peasant constantly below poverty, but helped to maintain the other sections in relative affluence.

Besides, the Kashmiri peasant was ruled by customs (Rewaj) and traditions. It was very difficult for the peasant to maintain a subsistence level when he had to spend expensively on occasions of marriage, birth, death and other religious and social ceremonies.[69] The peasantry comprised different groups which belonged to various religions and castes. In a study of the peasantry of Kashmir, one comes across the peculiar feature namely the absence of rigidity in caste system, which among other things distinguishes it from other regions of India. Caste system had become quite flexible except for Pandits and Peers.[70] Perhaps the utter poverty at the lower ends of society, which compelled the poor of all castes to supplement their income from land by various other means, introduced an element of flexibility in the caste-system.

Hence from the foreging account the peasantry of Kashmir appears to have been constantly dipped into poverty and starvation It was all as a result of the combined effects of the natural and men made calamities. On the one hand there prevailed low level of production as a result of backward agricultural technology and inadequate irrigation, on the other hand the increasing tax burden went on casting darker shadows over the prospects of peasantry.

---

69. Lawrence, Valley, pp. 256-61. See also Administrative Report of Jammu and Kashmir State, 1921-22, Jammu, 1923, p. 28.
70. The *nongars* (non-agriculturists) could take to agriculture easily. Even village menials could indulge in agriculture and rank themselves with agricultural classes in society. Because land was the determining factor in society, there was no caste barrier, Lawrence, *Valley*, pp. 305-306.

The only means to escape from all these problems found by the peasantry was to flee to other parts of the country but that was no real escape.

6
Pattern of Trade

Besides agriculture, trade and industrial activity though on a very limited scale, constituted another means of livelihood for Kashmir's population. But until the end of the 19th century internal and external trade of Kashmir was not based on any sophisticated network of local markets. Bad roads, inadequate communication, a variety of weights and measures and poor administrative and financial system, all impeded trade in and outside the country.[1]

So far as trade in argicultural products was concerned the limited nature of production and technical backwardness did not aid its expansion. It was the State alone which played the role of the grain trader in Kashmir.[2] To that end the State annually collected a good number of *kharwars* of grain in the form of land revenue and various other cesses and stored the grain in the State stores, until the

1. During Maharaja Gulab Singhs period there were two kinds of weights and measures. The weights of stone were introduced. One kind among these was used for official dealings the other was used to defraud the people. Mirza, *op.cit.*, Vol. I, f. 113.
2. Mirza, *ibid.*, ff. 1. 27, 36. Foreign and Pol. July 1863, file nos. 73-75, N.A.I. See also M.I. Khan, *History of Srinagar*, Srinagar, 1978, pp. 57-58.

Government stock from these state stores was sold, the grain merchants throughout the valley were not allowed to engage in trade. If at all they intended to do so, they had to purchase their stock from the Government which they could market.[3] To prevent any infringement of this order, grain was sold out in small quantities not only to the grain dealers but even to the needy. The State had the fear that if the people, particularly in towns, were left with surplus grain, they might sell it at high rates and encourage the grain trade at the hands of grain dealers.[4] In view of this rice sufficient only for fifteen days consumption was sold at a time. Capt. Cunnigham, who visited Kashmir during Maharaja Gulab Singh's reign observed, "It is impossible to obtain so much as one rupee worth of wheat in city of Kashmir. Not more than five or six seers could be purchased at one time and this was considered to be a great hardship by the middle class who had been accustomed to buy wheat sufficiently".[5]

On the other hand, the State demand was collected in kind for most of the time, the State had arbitrarily reserved to itself the right of fixing the market rates. Under this system the peasants were not left with enough food for the whole year and consequently they had to purchase it form the market like all other non-cultivating sections of population.[6] This system made peasant families dependent on money.[7] The State virtually enjoyed monopoly of trade

---

3. Capt. Cunnigham, *memo,* Foeign Deptt. Sec. 31 March 1848, file nos. 66-77, N.A.I. Lawrence, *Valley,* pp. 390-94.
4. Lawrence, *Valley,* p. 23.
5. Capt. Cunnigham, *memo.*
6. *Ibid.* R.H. Davis, *The Report on Trade and Resources of Countries on the north western boundary,* Lahore, 1862, pp. 47-49. *Foreign and Pol.* A July 1863, file No. 73-75, N.A.I., Lawrence, *Valley,* pp. 39-94.
7. Lawrence, *Valley,* pp. 390-94.

in food grains.[8] The movement of food grains inside the village and town was associated with long established modes of economic domination and exploitation.[9] The main aim of the peasants was naturally to grow food crops and to feed themselves. But their fortune was linked to the urban areas where they had to feed the lords, the State's functionaries and other non-cultivating sections of the population among whom the majority was of shawlweavers.[10] Hence in one way or the other they had to part with most of their food crops and obtained in return a bit of iron, salt and cloth. Some of the peasant proprietors, who possessed grains in addition to their subsistance requirement, used to carry that to the Punjab, Rawalpindi and other areas in northern India, in exchange for salt and clothes.[11] It was not merely the monopolistic policy of the State that did not permit the grain merchants to stand between the actual producer and the market. Kashmir lacked the modern means of communication and transport. Even as late as 1890 W.R. Lawrence wrote,"one of points which at once strike a visitor to Kashmir is absence of roads fit for wheeled carriage... The roads as understood in other countries do not exist."[12] Some of the agricultural and

---

8. There was no open market for food grains and as such open market operations were absent. It was, therefore, a question of people purchasing whatever the State had to sell at a rate, that was arbitrarily fixed by the State.
9. The state itself was the dominating party in food procurement and trade. The regulation of the whole operation was arbitrary and as such it provided extensive scope for exploitation of various sections of society, particularly the landless peasants.
10. Mirza, *Akhbarat*, Vol. I, ff. 1-2.
11. R.H. Davis, *op. cit.*, Appendix A., pp. 1-30. *Majmu-i-Report of Jammu Kashmir-va-Tibet*, 1873-75. See also *Memorandum on Central Asia and its trade with Hindustan by Capt. T.G. Montigomerie to the Secretary to Govt. of Punjab* No. 173, July 20, 1861, N.A.I.
12. Lawrence, *Valley*, p. 23.

pastoral products such as wool, barley, hides, drugs, oil seeds, wood and other cereals which should have served a variety of useful purposes could not be transported to urban areas in handsome quantities. Besides the want of capital and absence of enterprise on the part of grain merchants. There were other constraints which hampered the development of trade beyond a certain limit during the period of our study.[13] The chief items of export and import were as follows:

Imports	Exports
Raw cotton, piece goods, brass, iron, salt, sugar tobacco and snuff.	Drugs, raw fibres, fibres manufactured, fruits, skins and hides, oil seeds, wool, shawls and woolen piece goods.[14]

Among the articles of export drugs, fibres, fruits and woolen piece goods were of chief importance not only to the traders but also to the peasants in general. The lack of statistical figures in our sources presents great difficulty in determining the actual volume of trade in agricultural products. However, the following table shows the rupee value of these articles of export trade for the years from 1886 to 1893.[15]

---

13. In fact this development in transport should have easily exposed Kashmir to the world at that time when rapid industrial development was taking place almost in every part of the world. Europe was making advances in science and technology. Industry was superseding agriculture as the main source of livelihood for a majoriry of people. But Kashmir remained primitive in its self-imposed isolation.
14. Capt. Cunnigham, *memo*. R.H. Davis, *op. cit*, pp. 47-49. *The Foreign and Pol.* A., July 1863, file No. 73-75, N.A.I. Lawrence, Valley, pp. 390-94.
15. Lawrence, *Valley*, pp. 390-94.

Article	*1886-87*	*1887-88*	*1888-89*	*1889-90*	*1890-91*	*1891-92*	*1892-93*
Drugs	178843	247016	261016	209571	340672	407969	160625
Fibres	6279	14861	13466	10245	10435	11570	8919
Fruits	141485	257542	243501	301068	227782	222645	236683
Woolen piece goods	593257	549463	600729	717721	637522	511235	591439

The given table suggests the meagreness of the volume of exports even though there was a marginal increase in the export volume. The drugs included *chob-i-kuth,* lac, leaves of *kah-i-zaban* (Macrolomia banthrui) and the leaves and seed of Hyonrcyanuis, Niger, Henbane and other medicinal plants and flowers.[16] There were collected by the peasants from forests which they handed over to local shopkeepers in return for tea and salt.[17]

Kashmir also appears to have exported a great quantity of woollen piece goods to other regions like Punjab and other parts of Central Asia.[18]

Utilization of fruits for commercial purposes appears to have increased during the period of our study. Being a perishable commodity and due to lack of quick means of transport, the fruits could not be exported to far off markets. Among fruits walnuts, apple and grapes had some demand in the market. Walnuts were used for extracting oil by *wanies*

16. Among these medicinal plants and flowers the roses were very important because they were made into jam *(Khimbeer)* and then exported to the Punjab. It was as a result of this that Maharaja Gulab Singh got some of the places converted into rose gardens like the western bank of *Kut-Kul* canal where mainly roses were grown. Mirza, *op. cit,* Vol. iv, p. 88.
17. *Ibid.* See also Lawrence, *Valley,* pp. 390-94.
18. R.H. Davis, *op. cit.,* Appendix A. pp. 1-3, *Majmu-i-Report of Jammu, Kashmir-va-Tibet,* 1873-75. See also, *memorandum on Central Asia and its trade with Hindustan by Capt. T.G. Montigomerie to the Secretary to Govt. of Punjab,* No. 173, 20 July, 1861, N.A.I

TABLE 8

The given table shows the total sales of wine from 1882 to 1900 in bottles.[19]

Year	White Wine	Red Wine	No.1 Brandy	No.2 Brandy	Apple Brandy	Vinejar	Spirits of Wine	Cider	Absinthe	Chem-pagne and Cinchona	Cheery Brandy	Total
1882-83	-	841	-	113	3996	36	-	-	-	-	-	4976
1883-84	750	1778	-	13	5894	44	-	-	-	-	-	8479
1884-85	880	1448	6	194	5736	70	-	-	-	-	-	8342
1885-86	194	98	2	98	7144	52	48	-	-	-	-	7336
1886-87	639	1024	1	4	4708	109	-	-	-	-	-	6485
1887-88	1455	4803	-	166	11722	109	-	-	-	-	-	18257
1888-89	880	2091	60	26	10055	98	-	-	-	-	-	13210
1889-90	1208	2832	122	209	16448	27	-	-	-	-	-	20846
1890-91	1218	4663	81	129	14197	1	-	-	-	-	-	20294
1891-92	723	3307	69	157	14764	57	-	-	-	-	-	19077
1892-93	903	3814	49	417	17298	61	28	-	-	-	-	22579
1893-94	1347	3082	109	417	16322	175	67	59	-	15	-	21578
1894-95	879	5271	185	436	18462	363	57	799	-	-	-	26467
1895-96	1162	3578	77	394	16482	158	122	351	-	-	-	22324
1896-97	1126	3671	190	259	22576	85	626	160	-	-	-	28193
1897-98	1650	4666	166	229	19864	200	199	419	-	-	26	27516
1898-99	2190	7078	141	288	23323	126	222	659	-	6	70	34103
1899-1900	1720	6870	139	317	25760	105	233	1077	194	7	225	36547

19. The given figures have been collected from the Administrative Reports of the period from 1882-1900 which are available in State Archives at Jammu and Srinagar.

TABLE 9

This table shows the total cash realized from the year 1882-1900 from wine sales

Year	White Wine	Red Wine	No.1 Brandy	No.2 Brandy	Apple Brandy	Spirits of wine	Wine jar	Cider	Anisette & absinthe	Cham-pagne & cinchona	Cherry Brandy	Mis-cell-aneous	Total receipt
1882-83	-	853	-	158	2293	-	13	-	-	-	-	-	3317
1883-84	756	1848	-	22	4681	-	25	-	-	-	-	-	7332
1884-85	948	1810	18	366	4072	72	38	-	-	-	-	-	7252
1885-86	328	196	6	183	5043	-	22	-	-	-	-	-	5860
1886-87	643	1373	3	10	2742	-	18	-	-	-	-	-	4789
1887-88	1422	4000	-	200	9000	-	90	-	-	-	-	-	14712
1888-89	1001	2370	176	52	5972	-	57	-	-	-	-	-	9628
1889-90	1400	4000	334	353	9850	-	25	-	-	-	-	-	15140
1890-91	1362	2370	235	245	11353	-	1	-	-	-	-	-	18432
1891-92	792	3178	199	296	11990	-	35	-	-	-	-	-	16787
1892-93	996	5236	146	815	13445	42	53	-	-	-	-	-	19872
1893-94	1286	3475	309	789	14776	85	106	18	-	-	-	462	20772
1894-95	827	4375	494	804	14263	72	218	250	-	30	-	378	22396
1895-96	1106	2940	214	745	14005	152	98	110	-	-	-	136	20400
1896-97	1098	5062	527	489	17458	158	53	50	-	-	-	156	23927
1897-98	1447	3834	458	624	17281	294	125	131	-	-	52	558	25689
1898-99	1866	3938	388	550	19278	277	79	220	-	18	139	301	30746
1899-1900	1613	4766	383	612	22446	291	66	340	177	21	450	501	34603

TABLE 10

This table shows the Bottles departmentally used and the Dryage

			Dryage			
Year	*Departmentally used No of Bottles*	*White Wine*	*Red Wine*	*Brandy*	*Total Dryage*	*Total*
1882-83	1172	-	-	25	25	1197
1883-84	450	-	-	4	4	454
1884-85	335	-	-	-	-	335
1885-86	462	1500	-	541	2041	2503
1886-87	1909	547	243	126	915	2824
1887-88	470	685	352	3	1040	1510
1888-89	434	784	593	1308	2685	3199
1889-90	1674	1727	1681	2	3410	5084
1890-91	634	1666	1286	3	2955	3589
1891-92	806	1455	929	8608	10992	11798
1892-93	640	2741	1707	6555	11003	11643
1893-94	1841	1829	3671	938	6438	8279
1894-95	7416	2492	387	1122	4001	11447
1895-96	7304	3242	1531	1245	6018	13322
1896-97	1822	3089	1421	1065	5575	7307
1897-98	27530	696	372	2940	4008	31338
1898-99	278	1677	1577	1715	4969	5247
1899-1900	635	1539	1901	1712	5152	5787

TABLE 11

The following table shows the details of expenditure on Wine Industry from 1882-1900

Year	*Building*		*Machinery etc.*	*Establish-ment*	*Cropes*	*Apples*	*Miscellane-ous & Fuel*	*Total Exp-penditure*
	P.W.D.	*Civil Department*						
1882-83	-	-	2544	866	1000	2996	1103	8509
1883-84	-	-	3396	1439	1635	1893	954	9317
1884-85	-	-	2435	1804	2750	2450	1264	10703
1885-86	-	-	354	259	2053	190	283	3179
1886-87	-	-	2499	7605	2975	-	19	13098
1887-88	19480	-	7794	7488	4187	-	22	38971
1888-89	1367	24	6834	7917	-	-	-	16142
1889-90	5561	-	2326	7297	1534	-	2333	19951
1890-91	912	10	919	6731	1296	67	1587	11522
1891-92	228	150	2856	5427	3760	-	3039	15460
1892-93	1185	-	-	6435	627	-	7259	15516
1893-94	-	-	-	7072	2574	-	4537	14177-
1894-95	5547	-	-	7831	2300	2310	2802	23790
1895-96	520	-	1530	7975	44	371	5713	16153
1896-97	-	-	-	9701	4271	2246	5885	22103
1897-98	509	-	3830	10483	1351	120	3738	20031
1898-99	22	-	160	10275	199	1236	2566	15458
1899-1900	437	-	200	10386	1474	2952	2921	15370

and *bakals* who provided the agricultural population or the sellers of fruits with snuff, iron implements, tobacco, cotton piece goods and some amount of sugur.[20]

During Maharaja Ranbir Singh's period the perishable commodity of fruit like grapes and apples assumed a commercial significance, when a wine distillery and wine manufactory were founded in Kashmir for manufacturing wine from grapes and apples.[21] However, the extent to which these products were commercialized can be seen from the following table which gives the total sales and total expenditure incurred from 1882 to 1900 A.D.[22]

So far as other agricultural products like saffron, waternuts and oil seeds are concerned, our sources do not figure out the volume of saffron and waternuts exported during the period under study. The cash value of oil seeds exported from 1886 upto 1893 is as follows.[23]

Kind	*1886-1887*	*1887-1888*	*1888-1889*	*1889-1890*	*1890-1891*	*1891-1892*	*1392-1393*
Linseed	1766	660	627	6201	18528	5479	1335
Mustard and rape	9114	13893	35673	81189	13491	99624	59769
Till	12140	35283	16000	47160	82941	29644	107024

The forest produce particularly wood which was in great demand in India for construction of railways but due to the absence of technical know-how and modern means of transport it could not be exploited on desired scale.[24] The

20. Lawrence, *Valley*, pp. 390-94.
21. Pandit Bhag Ram, *Annual Administration Report of Jammu and Kashmir*, 1893, Jammu, 1894, pp. 130-131.
22. M. Suraj Bal, *Administration Report of Jammu and Kashmir*, 1898-1900, Jammu, 1901, pp. 303-323.
23. Lawrence, *valley*, p. 383.
24. Sir R. Temple, *India in 1880*, London 1881, pp. 296-99. See also *A Note on Jammu and Kashmir State*, pp. 41-45.

following table shows the value of exported wood from 1886 upto 1893 in Rupees.[25]

1886-1887	*1887-1888*	*1888-1889*	*1889-1890*	*1890-1891*	*1891-1892*	*1892-1893*
185914	289333	253765	48282	43890	202124	49696

Shawl and Silk Trade

Shawl and silk industry also provided occupation to Kashmir's population. The shawls of Kashmir were highly praised not only in India but in the royal courts of France, England and other countries of the world.[26]

For manufacturing shawls the pashm (wool) of the domesticated goat and *Asli Tus* (The finer wool of wild goat) was imported from Chanthan, Yarkand, Khutan, Tibet, Chinese Turkistan and some other parts of Central Asia.[27]

The shawl manufacture had to undergo a long apprenticeship before acquiring the shape of finished product. First the women would pick the coarse hairs from the imported wool. In this process 1/3 of the weight was lost and the remainder was packed in layers with rice flour slightly moistened with oil and was subjected to a pressure under stone for about 48 hours, whereby it was cleaned and spun into thread by women.[28] After the process of cleaning and spinning of raw material was over it was then taken to

25. Lawrence, *op. cit.*, p. 388.
26. Charles Girdlestone, *op. cit.*, pp. 29-30.
27. Mirza, *op. cit.*, Vol.I, ff. 93, 96. R.H. Davis, *op. cit,.* pp. 48-49, and Appendix XXIV. *Foreign see. Sept. 1872* file No. 59, N.A.I. *Charles* Girdlestone, *op. cit.*, p. 30.
28. *Foreign and Pol.* A. March 31, 1848, File Nos. 66-70, N.A.I. All the peasants of Kashmir were engaged by the state officials for cleaning this wool without wages. Mirza, *op. cit.*, Vol. I, ff. 93-96.

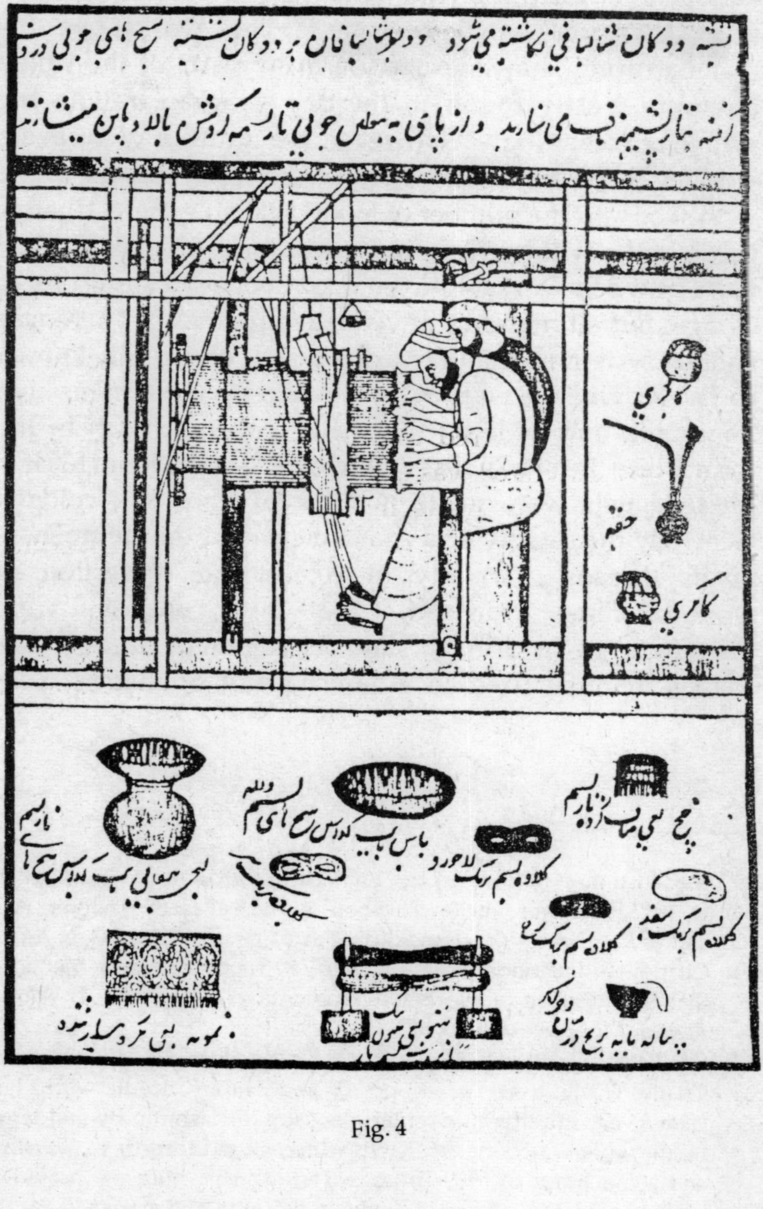

Fig. 4

karkhanas or factories, where the weavers used to weave it into shawl on wooden looms.[29] The workshops for manufacturing shawls existed in many parts of the valley but were mostly found in the city of Srinagar with the primitive technology.[30] However, the number of weavers working in the *karkhanas* varied according to the size of the workshop and the number of looms available there. Charles Girdlestone, who visited Kashmir in the 1870s says. "The most crowded workshop contained about sixty persons of all ages but all males in ill-ventilated rooms".[31] There was another system of manufacturing shawls commonly known as *Sadabaf*, where a weaver used to spin *pashmina* in his own house and embroidered the shawl with needles.[32] In the former case the shawl was embroidered on the loom itself.[33] These shawls were made in different sizes and colours. Generally the quality of a shawl depended on the fineness of its threads, harmony of colour and prefection of workmanship. However, the best shawls were manufactured in Srinagar and its adjoining areas.[34] The shawls manufactured in Anantnag and Shahabad were

---

29. See illustration following page 206. Charles Girdlestone, *op. cit.*, p. 28.
30. In 1847 there were 6000 workshops in the valley of Kashmir. *R.G. Taylors Regulations, (Ain) for.sec. cons.* dated January 28, 1848, N.A.I.
31. Charles Girdlestone, *op. cit.*, pp. 28-29. R. Thorp, however, mentions that the number of workmen ranged from 20 to 300. T. Thorp, *Kashmir Misgovernment*, p. 62.
32. C.E. Bates, *Gazetteer*, p. 54, see also M.I. Khan *History of Srinagar*, p. 56.
33. Charles Girdlestone, *op. cit.*, pp. 28-29. *Sozankari* (needle work) has been a very important subsidary industry of Kashmir. By and large needle work was done on shawls with coloured threads of *pashmina* and some times of *Tila* (Brocade Thread) This industry provided work to a sizeable section of Kashmiri peasants, and artisans.
34. *Ibid.*, p. 28.

inferior to those of Srinagar.[35] Generally the shawl was woven the wrong side and was rolled on wooden beam from which it seldom turned perfect. The shortcomings if any were removed by hand. After this work was over, the shawl was passed into the hands of local washerman who took the responsibility of removing the dirt and in adding it a true shape for landing in the market.[36]

In 1870s the price of best shawls varied from Rs. 350 to 1800, the square ones fetched Rs. 200 to 1200.[37] From 1862 to 1870 the export value of shawls averaged between 25 and 28 lakhs of Rupees.[38] The export value of shawls for the years from 1886 to 1893 will be clear from the following table.[39]

1886-1887	*1887-1888*	*1888-1889*	*1889-1890*	*1890-1891*	*1891-1892*	*1892-1893*
1210012	1268500	607510	708300	196250	85250	219275

The given table reveals a steady decrease in export of shawls. There were several reasons for this decline. In the twenty years preceding 1871, Europe which provided brisk market for Kashmiri shawls, was shaken by no less than five wars each involving two or more great powers of the

35. *Ibid.*, pp. 28-29. The village workman did not have these facilities which were available to the urban artisans who worked in intimate touch with top businessmen and exporters. Moreover, the village artisan was essentially either a landed or landless peasant who pursued the profession of shawl making only to subsidize his income. As such he did not possess rich tradition of workmanship which was the privilege of urban craftsmen.
36. *Ibid.*, pp. 28-30. See *Foreign and Pol. A., March* 31, 1848, File Nos. 60-70 (Capt. Cunnigham's *Memo on Kashmir*), N.A.I.
37. Charles Girdlestone, *op. cit.*, p. 28.
38. R.H. Davis, *op. cit.*, See Appendix CCV-CCXX.
39. W.R. Lawrence, *Valley*, p. 388.

world.[40] All these wars put a stop to the shawl trade of Kashmir. No reports were available about the international market and there was a general impression that no dealing involving the shawl trade may be entered into. To quote F. Younghusband, "Kashmiri shawls in the middle of last century (19th) used to be very fashionable in Europe but the Franco-Prussian war of 1870-71 seems to have sealed the fate of the industry. After 1870 the fashion went out and has never revived and famine of 1877-79 carried off numbers of weavers so that now very few carry on the industry."[41]

Another factor that appears to have restricted the growth of industry was the fiscal obstruction. In 1852 the total taxes collected on *Dag Shawl* (the shawl Department) amounted to 7,50,00 rupees.[42] The manufacturers has not only to pay stamp duty but also custom duty on export.[43] According to R. Thorp, 47.8% was the duty annually levied on individual weaver.[44] John Irvin says that advalorem duty of 25% was charged on each shawl and its assessment and collection were farmed out to corrupt body of officials, whose illegal exactions were said to have amounted to further 25% of the value.[45] According to R.H. Davis till 1868 Rs. 30 were annually demanded from weavers.[46] In 1868 this demand was reduced to Rs. 23/- but still the impost of 20% was levied per head.[47]

---

40. W.K. Farguson and G. Brun, *A Survey of European Civilization*, Boston, p. 738. All these wars—the Crimean War, the Italian war of 1859, the Danish war, the Austro-Prussian conflict and the Franco-Prussian war–speeded up the tension which proved harmful for trade throughout the period.
41. F. Youghusband, *Kashmir*, p. 211.
42. Mirza Saif-ud-Din., *Akhbarat*, Vol. I, f. 24.
43. *Ibid.*
44. R. Thorp, *Kashmir Misgovernment*, p. 63 (typed copy).
45. John Irwin, *The Kashmir Shawl*, London, 1955, p. 9.
46. R.H. Davis, *op.cit.*, p. 73.
47. Charles Girdleston, *op.cit.*, p. 29.

R. Maclagan observes, "From annexed reports it is painfully evident that owing to the narrow minded and suicidal policy of the Kashmir ruler an enormous decrease in the trade between Punjab and Kashmir has taken place. The duty levied amounts almost to prohibition, and to make matters worse the Maharaja endeavours to force trade through a certain channel. Such a policy could not fail to affect the trade disadvantageously".[48] Hence the taxes charged were no less serious a burden for the weaver population who showed lack of interest and consequently the production fell through.

The worst feature of the industry which appears to have given due allowance to its decline was the condition of workers. The nearest and the most important evil oppressing the weavers was the utter lack of hope of ever rising from their depressed condition. The more oppressive burden weighing on the weavers was the insecurity of employment. The badly constructed houses and workshops undermined their physical condition. What care or education could be given to children where their parents were working in *Karkhanas* for more than 12 hours a day and how was it possible to share life under one roof when members of the family were kept away from the home all day by their work and hardly met at all except when it was time to got to bed.[49] Surveying the multitude of deleterious influences affecting the health of weavers we can readily draw conclusions about their physical condition. Lack of care during the first years of life, insufficient and poor food, unhealthy housing conditions, inadequate clothing in severe winter, insufficient protection against the vagaries of

48. "Memorandum of R. Maclagan, Secretary to the Government of Punjab", *Davis, Report,* Appendix. E.
49. Charles Girdlestone, *op.cit.,* pp. 28-30.

weather lack of medical assistance and nursing care in sickness, finally the pre-mature employment of children in occuption deleterious to their development.[50] These were the common causes of generally stunted physical condition of workers. Moreover, most places of work were arranged without any consideration for workers' help, quite apart from the fact that industrial occupations and overwork were in themselves harmful to health. Charles Girdlestone very rightly remarks, "The occupation of shawl weavers is hereditary, more from compulsion than choice, for the son seems to have no option but to follow in his fathers footsteps."[51] The weavers were paid very small wages which were calculated according to the number of sticks of pashm thread prepared by each. One who could work the stick in woof and warf one thousand times, was reckowned to have performed work worth one stick. Accordingly the daily wages of Weavers averaged between two and six annas.[52] In 1847 the shawl weavers abandoned the work and made representation to the Maharaja for their inadequate wages.[53] In 1854 when Maharaja Gulab Singh felt that *karkhanas* were emptied by exodus of shawl weavers, he decided to pay 2½ annas more than their usual wages but only when the shawls were in great demand. Otherwise this increase of 2½ annas was liable to reduction during years of lean demand. This was opposed by weavers and finally an increase of 1¼ annas was made in their wages.[54]

---

50. *Ibid.*, See also C.E. Bates, *Gazetteer*, p. 33. Hassan, *op.cit.*, Vol. III (Urdu tr.) p. 572. Sir R. Temple, *Journals kept in Hyderabad, Kashmir, Sikkim and Nepal*, 2 vols. 1859-71, London, 1887, p. 276.
51. Charles Girdlestone, *op.cit.*, p. 28.
52. Ganesh Dass, *Sayahatnama*, p. 33.
53. Mirza Saif-ud-Din, *Akhbarat*, Vol. I, f. 21.
54. *Ibid.*

The *kitabwals* or *ustad* who kept account of wages of weavers and taught patterns earned from six to eight annas a day.[55] He received two annas for his general supervision work including account keeping. In addition to it he was paid one anna and three pie per square shawl and one anna per striped and per flowered piece.[56] For coloured pattern the weavers got two pies.[57] These wages were not paid in coin but in kind. They were provided with paddy which was their staple food.[58]

Silk

Though silk industry was of long standing in Kashmir during the period under study, the industry appears to have been neither promising nor paying. Maharaja Gulab Singh entrusted the charge of silk industry to Hakim Azim, his court physician.[59] The scattered references regarding the production of silk are not sufficient to generalize that the industry witnessed some advancement during Maharaja Gulab Singh's reign.[60]

It was in fact during Maharaja Ranbir Singh's time that silk industry was reorganised. Filature was imported from Europe with different kinds of silkworm eggs and a department was established for undertaking developmental activities. 127 rearing houses were established in different parts of the valley. However, the industry was not fully equipped to protect itself from different calamities both natural and man made. In 1878 A.D. all the silk worms

55. Charles Girdlestone, *op.cit.*, p. 29.
56. *Ibid.*
57. *Ibid.*
58. Mirza Saif-ud-Din, *Akhbarat*, f. 30.
59. G.M.D. Sufi, *Kashir*, Vol. II, p. 575.
60. *Ibid.*

were carried off by disease.[61] Though the supervision of Industry was entrusted to Babu Nilamber Mukerjee, improvement in reeling of silk and improvement in its production remained a far fetched thing. No doubt in 1881 Mr. Prakash Joo was able to procure some seed through Mr. Johnson who had gone to visit yarkand in this connection.[62] Again the symptoms of disease appeared and worms died. From 1882-1890 various experiments were carried out to make this industry a going concern but unfortunately the whole concern was left in the hands of silk reares who did not posses the managerial skill to ensure its progress.[63]

The number of rearing houses shrank and only two survived, one in cherpura and the other in *Ragu Nath Pora.*[64] In 1889 attempts were made to import seeds from Italy and France on the advice of Sir Adward Buck, Secretary to the Government of India.[65] In the same year Sir Thomas Wardles services were obtained to give industry some amount of strength but till the end of 19th century the industry remained merely in an experimental stage and not a commercial enterprise. Originally all the process in the production of raw silk were conducted in the peasant household. The farmers and their families grew the mulberry trees, reared the silkworms in sheds attached to their houses and reeled the silk on traditional instruments.[66] The experiments which were carried out one after the other could not set the industry at once to the task of meeting a large foreign demand both for silk worm eggs and silk in

---

61. Pt. Anand Koul, *Geography of Jammu and Kashmir State,* p. 58.
62. *Ibid.*
63. Lawrence, *Valley,* p. 368.
64. *Ibid.* See also S.T. Wardle, *Kashmir, its new Silk Industry,* London 1904, p. 35.
65. Pt. Anand Koul, *op. cit.*, p. 58.
66. *Dewan Krishen Lal's Account of Kashmir,* Foreign Sec. 31st March, 1848, file nos. 66-77.

consequence of the outbreak of silk worm disease in Europe. No boubt, it was taken up by increased number of peasants but that did not help the expansion of industry.[67] Inspite of all these measures silk rearing remained a household industry in peasants hands. The rude methods employed by the peasants could not change the character of industry. There prevailed unhygenic conditions in the houses of peasants who were engaged in silk rearing. This consequently proved harmful for the insect.[68]

The officials employed from time to time never cared to see whether or not the instructions were faithfully implemented. The price of cocoons was never remunerative enough to ensure any success of the industry.[69] Besides the external backwardness of the silkworm rearing also effected the working of industry. The State never inculcated among the peasants the interest that mulberry was more paying. No moral pressure was used to influence the peasants to preserve used it more for fuel than for leaf.[70] Another reason for its under-development was the policy followed by the State, whatever little amount was annually realized was taken away by the Maharaja and the basic interest of the industry was ignnored due to lack of proper investment. To quote Lord Curzon, "The Maharaja and his

---

67. S.T. Wardle. *op.cit*, pp. 9-10. See also H.M. Gofery, *Report on an inquiry into the silk industry in India*, Vol. II, p. 40-41.
68. S.T.Wardle *op.cit.*, p. 237.
69. *Census of India*, 1921, Vol. XXII, Part I, pp. 178-179.
70. Manmohan Wazir, *The Silk Industry of Kashmir*, p. 96. See also Tara Chand Wazir, *My Life Story, the lesson it has taught me 77 years in Reprospect*, Vol.I, p. 293. Shri Tara Chand Wazir has worked in many capacities. He was Senior Sericulture Asset. in Sericulture Department of Kashmir from 1916-24. Deputy Director (1924-28). Director. (1931-41). Chief Director Sericulture (1942-48). The unpublished Autobiography is typed and available with his son Shri Man Mohan Wazir.

brother both strongly declaimed in Darbar assembled to meet me in Jammu in spring in 1903 against handing over of industry to private enterprise. It was a loosing concern under State because no profit was invested."[71]

Problem of Transport & Communication

Separated from Punjab by rocky mountain barriers, the territories of Kashmir were enconced in a way which cut them off from developments in plains for a considerable time. As a result of these long distance communication was difficult and scanty even within the valley. This life of forced seclusion was not conducive to the development of trade which could have contributed to the economy of a region as a whole.

The chief menas of carrying on trade was the human labour, "Man's back was considered superior to pack ponnies."[72] Porters, mules, donkeys, horses , bullocks and boats were employed for carrying goods from one place to other.[73]

The important commercial lines which connected Kashmir with the outside world were poonch route, the Murree route, the Pirpanjal route, the Kashmir Yarkand route and Muzzafarabad route.[74] The first among these routes which connected Srinagar and Deval via Baramulla was covered by boat upto Baramulla and thence forward from Baramulla to Rawalpindi by cart.[75] The second one was

---

71. S.T. Wardle, *op.cit.*, p. 237.
72. Major K. Mason, *Routes in Western Himalayas Poonch, Kashmir and Ladakh* , Vol I, Calcutta 1929, pp. 1-2.
73. *General Report on Kashmir Railway Survey*, 1890, Jammu Archives.
74. David Ross, *Land of five rivers and Sind*, London 1883, p. 147. R.H. Davis, *op.cit.*, Appendix XXIV. Lawrence, *Valley*, p. 383. See also *Imperial Gazetteer of India*, Vol. XV *from Kashmir to Kotayam*, p. 132.
75. Major K. Mason, *op.cit.*, Vol. I, pp. 1-18, 33-38, 144-146 for details see pages 234-293.

the most popular route which led from Srinagar to Bhimbar and thence to Gujarat. About 30 miles of distance from Bimbar to Gujarat was covered by cart.[76] The third route passed through Uri and reached Thana Mandi which lay at a distance of 70 miles from Bimbar.[77] Jammu was reached from Srinagar by a route which crossed Banihal pass.[78] The other routes which connected Kashmir with Punjab were from Amritsar to Jammu and thence to Banihal pass, from Amristar to Srinagar by Akhnoor and Bodtul pass.[79] The fourth route which connected Kashmir with Yarkand passed through Kargil and Leh.[80] The fifth one crossed through Baramulla and Muzaffarabad and Peshawar.[81] This was the principal route because Jammu was near to Amritsar, the then Emporium of the Punjab and partly because it remained open for more months during the year than other routes. But the route itself was not good. Horses could pass along with great difficulty.[82] The major portions of carriage were completed by men and pack bullocks.

All those routes which connected Kashmir with other countries were unsafe and in a very bad condition. On the Kashmir Yarkand route the depredations of robber tribe Koonjid and Kirgiz beyond the Karakoram range impeded trade.[83] Even during winter months these robbers did not spare the armed caravans of traders. The Yarkand

---

76. *Ibid.*, pp. 1-7.
77. *Ibid.* See also Lawrence, *Valley*, p. 383.
78. David Ross, *op.cit.*, pp. 139-40. Major K. *op.cit.*, pp. 33-38. See also Davis, *op.cit.*, Appendix XXIV.
79. *Imperial Gazetteer of India*, Vol XV, p. 74.
80. *Preliminary Report of Ladakh Settlement of 1908, p. 2, Assessment Report of Kargil Tehsil*, 1911, p. 35. Major K. Mason, *op.cit.*, Vol. I., pp. 234, 293.
81. Major K. Mason, *op.cit.*, Vol. I, pp. 75-80.
82. David Ross, *op.cit.*, pp. 139-40.
83. R.H. Davis, *op.cit.*, Appendix XXIV.

Government also did nothing to secure the merchants against the usual plundering on this route.[85] Though Maharaja Gulab Singh was compelled to send one Mr. Koodus Joo, a Kashmiri trader to *Akaskal* at Yarkand to arrange for the levy of duty for him at that place, so that these traders were protected on this Kashmir Yarkand route, Mr. Koodus Joo returned without much achievement. The *Akaskal* reported that nothing could be done until Maharaja Provided for safety of caravans from Kirgiz robbers.[85] During Maharaja Ranbir Singh's time Mr. Aziz Joo, a Munshi at the court of the Maharaja was sent to Yarkand with this object but the munshi was stopped at Yarkand chowki of police for six months and afterwards turned out of Yarkand with disgrace. Nothing was done to ensure security for traders on this route.

The routes which connected Kashmir with the Punjab were almost practically unusable. They remained closed for more than six months due to snow.[86] Only the Baramulla route used to remain open for most of the time in the year.

---

84. The Yarkand Government formerly levied a duty on all merchandize brought to Yarkand market and in return used to protect traders from all violence within its territories. After the invasion of Kashghar by Jahangir Khoja of Andeejan, the king of Kokan prevailed on the then Chinese Government to relinguish its right to duty levied on Yarkand traders from Kokan in his favour. The Chinese government, however, to escape the disgrade of such concession extended the exemption from levy of duty by Turkish Chinese Govt. to traders from all other directions. The Government of all countries trading with China, Yarkand and other parts of Central Asia made arrangements through their *Akaskai i.e.* (the head representative of traders) the Kashmiri *Akaskal,* however, could not make such arrangements in regard to the Kashmiri merchants. The Maharaja did not take immediate notice of it as a result trade declined due to insecurity. R.H. Davis. *op.cit.,* pp. CXCIV-CXCVI.
85. *Ibid.*
86. David Ross, *op.cit.,* pp. 139-140.

But it presented a lot of difficulty because the route was in a bad condition. Now whatever amount of trade could pass through these scanty and unfrequented roads with inadequate transport facilities, was restricted by the fiscal obstructions. The Maharaja and his officials demanded heavy amount of duties. These custom duties were annually farmed out to contractors who were among the Maharajas favourites.[87] During Maharaja Gulab Singh's time Pratap Shah of Rawalpindi was the contractor for custom and paid to the State twenty thousand rupees a year.[88]

During Maharaja Ranbir Singh's period Jammu, Banihal route was the main channel by which all the articles from Punjab with the exception of salt were imported to Kashmir.[89] Though duties on this route had slightly been lowered those on Akhnoor route, Bhimber and Muzaffarabad had been raised in no less than 38 cases.[90] No doubt large reductions were made on the direct route from Jammu to Leh by Sooroo but this was the worst and the least frequent route in the Maharaja's territories.[91]

Hence trade and industry did not register much improvement. The developmental activities in the matter of roads and transport could have easily opened up the country and brought it into direct contact with the world market.

---

87. *Copy of a letter from T.D. Forsyth to Esq. C.B.Commissioner and Superintendant Jullunder Division to T.H. Thornton Esq. D.C.L. Secretary to Government of Punjab*. Foreign and Pol. A. July 1863, file no. 73-75. N.A.I.
88. *Ibid*.
89. *Tr. of a petition submitted by Tara Chand, from Lahore to the Sacretary to the Punjab*. Govt. Foreign and Pol. A., Feb. 1867, file Nos. 26-27. N.A.I.
90. *Ibid*.
91. R.H. Davis. *op.cit*., XXIV.

Thus the combination of a number of factors such as geographical barriers, lack of proper incentives, exploitation of the artisans, heavy burden of taxes on trade and industry, insecurity of roads, difficulties in transport and technical stagnation and state monopolies, all proved detrimental to the growth and development of trade and industry in Kashmir.

7
Conclusion

In the foregoing pages we have analysed some chief aspects of Kashmir's agrarian history *viz.* agricultural production, the land revenue system, the position of the revenue assignees and grantees, the position of the peasantry in the rural society and the pattern of trade as the secondary sector of Kashmir's economy and society, in so far as it was related to the rural economy. Kashmir's agriculture was clearly primitive in the application of tools and techniques. The reasons for this are not far to seek. The climate hindered double cropping pattern; the region's isolation from the rest of the subcontinent gave it a degree of unchangeability that is far more marked than in other parts of India. The ruling class at various levels, smugly perpetuated this relative stasis by on the one hand taking no initiatives to improve upon the existing technology and on the other by exploiting the peasantry to the point of leaving it utterly resourceless to attempt improvement on its own.

No doubt the majority of the population depended on agriculture in Kashmir. That was also a highly stratified society and the social organization was perpetuating intense exploitation of the peasantry. But this stratification and exploitation did not provide any momentum for economic development and resulted in a large degree of stagnation of the society. Professor Harbans Mukhia has argued that in ancient and medieval Indian history, the high fertility of land and low subsistence needs of the peasantry eliminated those acute and prolonged conflicts from society which caused fundamental changes in the entire socio-economic organization in western Europe.[1] But this still does not explain satisfactorily the history of Kashmir. It is true that the fertility of land in the valley of Kashmir was very high and the subsistence of the peasant very low, though perhaps a shade higher than in the main land due to climatic factors. But the steady deterioration in the condition of the peasantry did not lead to any change in the production system. Nor did the change occur as a result of action from above at the level of State or the intermediaries.

The reasons for the production system not undergoing any change from above was the apathy of intermediaries and the State for developmental activities, because the intense exploitation met their timely needs. The form of payment and its amount that the peasant was obliged to make depended primarily on the arbitrary demands of revenue machinery.

The frequent assessments of revenue failed to bring either a settled advantage or a basic transformation in the economic relations of various classes connected with the land revenue administration. The landed intermediaries acted in an oppressive manner and gradually got transformed into a western type of landed proprietors. Besides, their demand for *begar* from the peasants resulted in the system of periodic migration of labour from Kashmir insearch of living, causing in turn a labour-shortage in Kashmir itself. They uprooted the Kashmiri peasant from

1. Harbans Mukhia, "was there Feudalism in Indian History?", The Journal of Peasant Studies, Vol. 3, No. 3, April 1981, pp. 292-93.

the sphere of his subsistence economy and forced him to cater to their own needs. This played a decisive role in the emergence of the wage labourer. From the second half of the 19th century down to the first half of the twentieth, the *begar* or forced labour system predominated all over Kashmir supported by the machinery of State. The Dogra intermediaries compelled the peasants to work in road building, transportation of goods, construction of administrative and private buildings for their own use.

The rate of extraction of revenue being high and the methods of collection being rigorous, whatever initiative and capital the peasantry might otherwise have had was sapped by the State. Peasantry, deprived of all resources above the barest subsistenee, and at times even below it, could not afford to increase productivity from their own lands and labour. To generate even the nascent capital for investment in the development of agriculture, the commercial activity would otherwise have been a suitable alternative for the peasants of State like Kashmir, which produced commercial fruit crops in abundance. But the success of such a system depended on well developed regional and wider markets as well as the means of communication and transport all of which were absent and the State evinced no interest in developing them.

On the other hand the monopoly of the State in the trade of agricultural and non-agricultural products with the consequent depression of prices paid to the peasants, brought him often to such levels where it was impossible for him to make a reasonable living.

The technological and economic stagnation of Kashmir in this period was thus the chief bottleneck in the region's social and economic development. The social context of the stagnation lay precisely in the high degree of exploitation of peasantry.

The exploitative nobility comprising the *chakdars*, the

jagirdars, the *pattadars,* and the *Muafiholders* were the main source of political and economic support for the Dogra Raj. They found that renting of land to peasants was more advantageous which also provided them a socio-economic basis for the phenomenon of wide-spread absenteeism among the landlords. The productive resources of Kashmir's land and labour were inadequately utilized in the first instance so that the landlord's exploitation of the peasant based as it was on limited production, perpetuated the backwardness of Kashmir's economy both for the peasant as well as the landlord.

Though a land settlement was undertaken in 1889 to give some relief to the peasantry and to ensure a redistribution of land, neither the revenue machinery nor the landed aristrocracy extended their cooperation for settling the agrarian problems, for it tended to delimit the opportunities for prerequisities and speculation.

Thus the land settlement of 1889, with all the best intentions, failed to register any progress either in the redistribution of land or in improving productivity. Kashmir during the second half of the nineteenth century provides us with a classic illustration of the elite in a backward society holding back the society's progress lest a change undermine its position.

Thus it is that while the neighbouring regions of Kashmir were, through various stages of internal and external turmoil, entering into the modern world, Kashmir retained most characteristics of a medieval economy and society down to the end of the nineteenth century, indeed, down to this day, though mercifully the winds of change have also been blowing over the past couple of decades.

Bibliography

I. PRIMARY SOURCES

A. Sanskrit and Persian Manuscripts and printed texts

Anonymous, *Tuhfat-ul-Ahbah,* Persian MS. Research Department Library, Srinagar, Kashmir. It deals with ancient history of Kashmir briefly but gives a detailed account of the religious and political activities of Sultans of Kashmir.

Dewan Amarnath, *Zafar nama-i-Ranjit Singh,* Persian MS. edited by Sita Ram Kholi, University of Punjab, Lahore, 1928. It is a detailed history of Maharaja Ranjit Singh and his political activities.

Ramju Dhar, *Kaifiat, Intizam Mulk-i-Kashmir,* Persian M.S. Research Department library Srinagar, Kashmir. This manuscript gives a short account of the revenue system of Kashmir from Emperor Akbar down to Maharaja Ranbir Singh's reign.

Abul Fazl, *Ain-i-Akbari,* 3 volumes English tr. of Vol. I by Blochmann and the two by H.S. Jarret which were further revised by Jadu Nath Sarkar. Oriental publisher Delhi 1974. Besides being an important source of Indian history *Ain-i-Akbari* provides us a detailed information on Kashmir's topography, the life of the people, the administrative system and the land revenue administration of Kashmir as a sarkar of the Mughal Empire.

Jona Raja, *Rajatarangini Sanskrit,* English tr. by J.C. Dutt 3 vols. Calcutta 1889. It is the earliest contemporary history of the Sultanate in Kashmir.

Pandit Kalhana, *Rajatarangini Sanskrit,* English translation by M.A. Stein, 2 vols., London, 1900. It is the first historical record of Kashmir. It is a rich store house of information on political, social, economic and cultural conditions of Kashmir from earliest times upto 1149-50.

Anonymous, *Tarikh-i-Kalan*, Persian MS. Punjab, State Archives Patiala. It is a detailed account about the Socio-economic and political condition of Kashmir under x sikhs. (1819-1846).

Ganeshi Lal, *Sayahat-nama*, Persian text, English translation by V.S. Suri Chandigarh, 1976. It is a brief but valuable account of Kashmir recorded by Ganeshi Lal during his visit to Kashmir in the 1840's.

Muhammad Khalil Mirjanpuri, *Tarikh-i-Kashmir*, Persian MS. Research Department Library Srinagar, Kashmir. It is a history of Kashmir from the earliest times upto Maharaja Ranbir Singh's reign. It was written under the orders of Raja Kak Dhar, one of the high officials of Maharaja Gulab Singh. It provides information on political economic and social problems of Kashmir from 1840 to 1885.

Dewan Kripa Ram, *Gulab-nama*, Persian text 'Lahore' 1865, English translation by S.S. Charak, Jammu, 1977. It is an official biogrphy of Maharaja Gulab Singh written by his Prime Minister under the orders of Maharaja Ranbir Singh.

Dewan Kripa Ram, *Gulzar-i-Kashmir*, Persian text, Lahore, 1877. The original manuscript is available in the National Archives of India, New Delhi. This book is a mine of information on Kashmir's agricultural and non-agricultural products. It throws a flood of light on technology which was used in carrying out agriculture and trade. It also gives detailed information about the various professions of Kashmir's population.

Mirza-Saif-ud-Din, *Akhbarat*, Persian MS. 13 vols. Research Department Library, Srinagar, Kashmir. It is a huge collection containing reports sent by Mirza Saif-ud-Din, the news writer of British Government at the court of Maharaja Gulab Singh. He used to send these reports to British authorities at Lahore. Besides providing information on social and economic aspects of Kashmir under Maharaja Gulab Singh, it also gives detailed information on Anglo-Kashmir relations from 1846 upto 1856.

Mir Saifullah, *Tarikhnama-i-Kashmir*, Persian Ms. The copy of this manuscript is available with the family of late Prof. Z.L. Jalla of Kashmir University, Srinagar. It provides a brief but interesting information on the socio-economic aspects of Kashmir under the Sikhs and the Dogras.

Peer Hassan Shah, *Tarikh-i-Kashmir*, Persian MS. 3 vols. 1885. Research Department Library Srinagar, Kashmir, Vol. I has been translated into urdu by Moulvi Mohd. Ibrahim and published from Srinagar in 1967. It is a detailed history of Kashmir from the earliest times down to the close of the 19th century. Besides political history it deals with the life of some saints of Kashmir. It is by for the most important and comprehensive work on the geography of Kashmir.

Anonymous, *Baharistan-i-Shahi*, Persian Ms. Research Department Library Srinagar, Kashmir. Though it describes the history of Kashmir from the earliest times, the information from the beginning of the Sultanate in Kashmir upto 1614 is more valuable.

B. Archival and Other Documents

The following documents have been consulted at the National Archives of India, New Delhi, Punjab State Archives, Patiala, Jammu and Kashmir State Archives at Srinagar and Jammu.

Mir Ahmed, *Dastural-Amal-i-Kashmir*, Parsian MS. M/829 Punjab States Archives Patiala. Besides dealing with the political aspects of Kashmir history it is an information sources on land revenue system of Kashmir under Afghan and Sikh rulers.

Arzi submitted by hill chiefs of Kashmir to Henery Lawrence, Foreign and secret consultations, December 26, 1846, file No. 1225, National Archives of India. *Copy of a letter from T.D. Forsyth C.B. Commissioner to T.H. Thronton secretary to Government of Punjab*. Foreign and political department A.

Feb, 1867 file Nos. 26-27, National Archives of India.

Capt. Cunnigham's Memo., Foreign and political department secret consultation 31 March, 1848, File Nos, 66-77, National Archives of India.

Chief secretariate, political and general department, 1876, Files No-76 Jammu Archives.

Foreign and political consultation, 30th December 1848 file No. 452-53, National Archives of India.

Foreign department section E, December 1890, File Nos. 196-211, National Archives of India.

Foreign department section E, File Nos. 295-306. National Archives of India.

R.P. Nisbets letter to the secretary government of India, Foreign department 29th January 1890, File No. 15, National Archives of India.

Foreign and political department, A. July 1863, file Nos. 73-75, National Archives of India.

Foreign department section E, October 1836, File Nos. 235-300, National Archives of India.

Foreign department secret consultation, December 1846, File Nos. 1266, National Archives of India.

Jammu and Kashmir State council proceedings, 26th October 1904 Jammu Archives.

Levy of Cesses in and reassessment of Jagirs in state and validity of pattas granted. Chief secretariate political and general department, file no. 76 of 1896, Jammu Archives.

H.M. Lawrence, *Transfer of Government to Maharaja Gulab Singh* section E, 28 January 1848, File No. 33-44, Jammu Archives.

W.R. Lawrence, *Report on the position of cultivating classes in Kashmir*, Foreign department section E, Feb. 1890, National Archives of India.

John Lawrence, *Condition of Kashmir*, Secret committee, 31 March 1848, File Nos. 66-77, National Archives of India.

Diary of P.S. Melvill, Punjab Government Records Lahore 1911-15, Punjab State Archives Patiala.

Dewan Krishan Lal, *Account of Kashmir,* Foreign department Section 31 March, 1848, File nos. 68, National Archives of India.

Diary of R.G. Taylor, Punjab Government Records (1847-49), Punjab State Archives Patiala.

H.L.P. Wynne, *Report on Kashmir,* 1872, Foreign and political department, January 1873, File nos. 343-349, National Archives of India.

Petition of Dewan Lachman Dass against the cash settlement, Chief secretariate Political and General Department, 1896, File no. 2, Jammu Archives.

Karvai-Jalsa-Council Aliya riyasat Jammu-va-Kashmir (Urdu and Persian), Jammu and Kashmir State Archives, Srinagar.

Khalsa Durbar Records vol. XIII No.3, Punjab State Archives, Patiala.

Letters from Sir Hentry Hardinge to Queen Victoria, Foreign and Political Department, 18 Feb. 1846, National Archives of India.

Farman regarding jagir. With cash and kind-in Martand and Devasar illaqa in favour of Pandit Raja Kak, Dhar 1905. Samvat. (with the family of Sham Sundar Lal Dhar in Boulvard at Srinagar.

Patta regading grant of jagir of Kava Chak illaqa on hereditary basis in favour of Pandit Raja Kak Dhar 1863, Photo State copy at Srinagar Archives.

Patta regarding grant of jagir in Nunar illaqa in favour of Pandit Raja Kak Dhar,1857 Jammu Archives.

C. Administrative, Assessment and other Reports

M. Suraj Bal, *Administrative Report of Jammu and Kashmir State,.* 1898-1900, Jammu 1901.

R.H. Davis, *The Report on Trade and resources of countries on north western boundary,* Lahore 1862, Jammu Archives.

H.M. Gofery, *Report on an enquiry into the Silk Industry in India,* Vol. II, National Archives of India.

W.R. Lawrence, *Assessment Report of Mirbahri,* Jammu 1898, Jammu, Archives.

——, *Assessment Report of Uri Tehsil,* Jammu 1898.

——, Assessment Report *of Pratap Singh Pora Tehsil* Jammu, Archives.

——, Asessmnet Report *of Ict, Nagam Tehsil,* Jammu, 1891.

——, *Assessment Report of Baramulla Tehsil*, Jammu, 1905.

Dewan Anant Ram, *Majmui-Report Jammu-va-Kashmir and Tibet.* (Urdu) (1873-75), Jammu, Archives.

Pandit Bhag Ram, *Annual Administration Report of Jammu and Kashmir State* (1889-90), Jammu, 1891.

——, *Annual Administration Report of Jammu and Kashmir State* (1890-91), Jammu, 1892.

——, *Annual Administration Report of Jammu and Kashmir,.* (1891-92). Jammu, 1893.

——, *Annual Administration Report of Jammu and Kashmir* (1892-93), Jammu, 1894.

——, *Annual Administration Report of Jammu and Kashmir State,* 1894-95, Jammu, 1896.

——, *Annual Administration Report of Jammu and Kashmir State,* 1895-96, Jammu, 1897.

——, *Annual Administration Report of Jammu and Kashmir State,* 1898-1900, Jammu, 1901.

Dewan Kripa Ram, *Majmui- Report on Jammu and Kashmir* (Urdu 1872-75), Jammu Archives.

General Report on Kashmir Railway Survey, 1890, Jammu Archives.

A Wingate, *Preliminary land settlement report in Kashmir*, Lahore, 1889.

Administrative Report of Jammu and Kashmir (1921-22), Jammu, 1923, (government publication)

A note on Jammu and Kashmir, Jammu, 1928, Jammu Archives.

Assessment Report of Kargil Tehsil, Jammu, 1911, Srinagar Archives.

Big Landed Estates Abolition Act., 1950, Srinagar 1950.

Big Landed Estates Abolition Act. XVII. *of Samvat*, 2007, Jammu, 1953.

Census of India 1921 Vol. XXII., Part I, Jammu, 1923.

R.G. Wreford, *Census of India*, 1941, Vol. XXII, Jammu 1943.

Report of British Empire Exhibition Jammu and Kashmir, London, 1924.

Wazir Gaganath, *Report on Jammu and Kashmir State*–1943, Jammu Archives.

W.R. Lawrence, *Assessment Report of Awantipura Tehsil,* Jammu 1920.

——, *Assessment report of Handware Tehsil*, Jammu, 1921.

Note on the review of the six Tehsils of the valley publish by Jammu and

Kashmir Government, Jammu, 1900.
Review of the working of the land reforms with special reference to big landed estates abolition act in Jammu and Kashmir, 1952.
Preliminary report of land settlement, Jammu, 1908.
Techno-Economic Survey of Jammu and Kashmir State, NCAER Delhi-1969.

D. Travel Accounts

A. L. Adams, *Wanderings of a naturalist in India*, Edinburgh, 1867.
Arthur Brinkman, *Wrong of Kashmir*, London, 1868.
Tyndale Biscoe, *Kashmir in Sunlight and Shade*, London, 1922.
G.C. Bruce, *Kashmir*, London, 1915.
G. Forester, *Selctions from Travels and Journals*, Bombay, 1909.
P. Grevis, *This is Kashmir*, London, 1954.
Charles Girdlestone, *Memorandum on Kashmir*, Calcutta, 1873.
C.B. Hugel, *The Punjab and Kashmir*, Jammu 1972, Second edition.
Victor Jacquemont, *Letters from India, London, 1936.*
J. Korbel, *Danger in Kashmir*, Srinagar, 1954.
E.F. Knight, *Where three empires meet*, London, 1905.
Capt. Knight, *Diary of a Pedestrain in Kashmir and Tibet*, London, 1863.
C.A. Lambert, *A trip to Kashmir and Ladakh, London, 1877.*
J. Milne, *The road to Kashmir*, London, 1929.
A. Neve, *Thirty years in Kashmir*, London, 1913.
W.F. Neve, *Beyond Pir Panjal*, London, 1915.
Maharaja Pratap Singh, *Diary of an inspection tour to Gilgit, Jammu, 1896.*
A. Petro Kokino, *Three weeks in a house boat*, Bombay, 1920.
R. Thorp, *Kashmir Misgovernment*, London, 1870.
W. Moorcraft and Trebeck, *Travels in Himalayan Provinces of Hindustan and Punjab, in Ladakh and Kashmir, 2 vols. London 1971, 2nd edition.*
W. Moorcraft, Tour Diary, Ms. EURD - 265 available in Jammu University Library.
David Ross, *Land of five rivers and Sind*, London, 1883.
G.T. Vigne, *Travels in Kashmir Ladakh, Iskardu, countries adjoining, the mountain courses of Indus and Himalayan*, North of Punjab, 2 vols, London, 1842.

F. Younghusband, *Kashmir*, Edinburgh, 1909.

E. Gazetteers

C.D.Bates, *A Gazetteer of Kashmir and Adjoining Districts of Kishtwar Badarwah, Jammu, Naoshers, Punch and the Valley of Kishenganga*, Calcutta, 1873.

Gazetteer of Kashmir and Ladak, Compiled under the Quarter Master General in India, the Intelligence Branch, Calcutta, 1890.

Imperial Gazetteer of India, Vol. XV (From Karachi to Kotayam), Oxford, 1908.

W.R. Lawrence, *Imperial Gazetteer of India, Provincial Series, Jammu and Kashmir*, Calcutta, 1909.

F. Contemporary Historical Works

F. Drew, *The Jammu and Kashmir Territories*. London, 1895.

- *The Northern Barrier of India*, London, 1877.

M.D. Fauq, *Rahnuna-i-Kashmir*, (Urdu) Lahore, 1912.

L.R. Griffin, *Punjab Chiefs*, Lahore, 1805.

Hargopal Koul Khasta, *Guldasta-i-Kashmir, Lahore, 1887.*

W.R. Lawrence, *Valley of Kashmir, London*, 1895.

S.C. Ray, *History and Culture of Kashmir*, Delhi, 1970, Second edition.

M.A. Stein, *Ancient Geography of Kashmir*, Calcutta, 1889.

Sir, R. Temple, *India in 1880*, London, 1881.

II. . SECONDRY SOURCES.

M. Athar Ali, *The Mughal nobility under Aurangzeb*, Aligarh, 1970.

P.N.K. Bamzai, *History of Kashmir, Political Social and Cultural*, Delhi-'1962.'

Indu Banga, *Agrarian System of the Sikhs*, Delhi, 1978.

S.S. Baw. *The Jammu Fox*, London, 1974.

M. Mohd. A.Beg, *Zarai-Islahat* (Urdu), Srinagar, 1950.

W. K. Ferguson and G. Bruun, *A Survey of European Civilization*, Boston, 1900.

B.N. Goswamy and J. S. Grewal, *Mughals and Jogis of Jakhabar*, Simla 1967.

Irfan Habib, *Agrarian System of Mughal India* (1526-1707), Bomby, 1963.

Guy Hunter, *Modernizing Peasant Societies*, Oxford London, 1969.

Fazal, Hussain, *Kashmir-aur-Dograraj*, Srinagar, 1979.

John Irwin, Kashmir Shawl, London, 1955

M.L. Kapoor, *A Socio-Economic History Maharaja Pratap Singh's Reign, 1885-1925*. Unpublished Ph. D. thesis approved by Jammu University in 1972.

S.N. Koul, *Kashmir Economics,* Srinagar, 1954.

S.R Koul, *Biography of Maharaja Gulab Singh,* Srinagar, 1923.

Pandit A. Koul, *Geography of Jammu and Kashmir,* Srinagar, 1980, Second edition.

D.D. Kosambi, *An introduction to the Study of Indian History,* Bombay 1956.

M.I. Khan, *History of Srinagar*, Srinagar, 1978.

S.M. Latif, *History of Punjab*, Delhi, 1964.

Major K. Mason, *Routes in Western Himalayas, Punch, Kashmir and Ladakh,* 2 vols, Calcutta, 1929.

Phool Pyari Mam, *Maharaja Gulab Singh,* an unpublished Ph. D. thesis approved by Kashmir University in 1981.

D. Nargis, *Tarikh-i-Dogra Desh,* Jammu, 1963.

——, *Maharaja Ranbir Singh,* Jammu, 1983

A.P. Nicholson, *Secrapes of Paper, India's broken treaties, her princes and her problem,* London, 1930.

K.M. Panikar, *Gulab Singh, the founder of Jammu and Kashmir State,* London, 1930.

R.K. Parmu, *History of Muslim Rule in Kashmir,* Delhi, 1969.

——, History of Dogra rule in Kashmir 1846-1947, unpublished Ms. consulted from Dr. R.K. Parmu, Director History Unit Jammu and Kashmir, Srinagar (Type copy)

D.K. Palit, *Jammu and Kashmir Arms,* Dehradun 1972, Bdan Porell *Land Systems of British India,* Delhi, 1967

A.N. Raina, *Geography of Jammu and Kashmir State,* Delhi, 1971.

S.M. Rai, *Partition of Punjab*, New York, 1965.

R.S. Sharma, *Indian Feudalism*, Calcutta, 1965.

R.L. Singh, *India a regional Geography,* Varanasi, 1971.

G.M.D. Sufi, *Kashmir,* 2 vols. Lahore, 1949.

A.N. Sapru, *The building of Jammu and Kashmir State, an achievement of Maharaja Gulab Singh,* Lahore, 1931.

S.F. Wardle, *kashmir and its new Silk, Industry* London, 1904.

T.C. Wazir, *My life story, the lession it has tought me 77 years in retrospect*. (Typed Ms. available with his son, Manmohan Wazir, Srinagar.

Elizabeth White Comb, *Agrarian Conditions in Northern, India*, Delhi, 1971.

INDEX